Of No Interest to the Nation

Of No Interest to the Nation

A Jewish Family in France, 1925–1945

A Memoir

GILBERT MICHLIN

With an Afterword by Zeev Sternhell

Wayne State University Press   Detroit

Originally published as *Aucun intérêt au
point de vue national: la grande illusion
d'une famille juive en France*

Manufactured in the United States of America.
08 07 06 05 04   5 4 3 2 1

Library of Congress Cataloging-in-Publication Data

Michlin, Gilbert, 1926–
[Aucun intérêt au point de vue national. English]

Of no interest to the nation : a Jewish family in France, 1925–1945 : a memoir /
Gilbert Michlin ; with an afterword by Zeev Sternhell. p. cm.
Includes bibliographical references.
ISBN 0-8143-3227-7 (pbk. : alk. paper)
1. Michlin, Gilbert, 1926–. 2. Jews—France—Biography. 3. Concentration camp
inmates—Biography. 4. Holocaust, Jewish (1939–1945)—France—Personal narratives.
I. Title.

DS135.F9M5313 2004
940.53'18'092—dc22

2004009641

∞The paper used in this publication meets the minimum requirements of the American
National Standard for Information Sciences—Permanence of Paper for Printed Library
Materials, ANSI Z39.48-1984.

To Riwka Dworetzkaia,
my dear mother

To Moshe-Meyer Michlin,
my dear father

To Mireille

To my brothers and sisters from Bobrek
(Auschwitz III)

CONTENTS

The Spark

I am one of the too numerous who experienced the German death camps during World War II. I am lucky to be one of the too few to have returned.

This monstrosity—this "experience," as it is usually referred to—is something I have never forgotten. To this day, I yearn to know why and how people could have plunged me into hell simply because I *was*. I yearn to understand why and how my father, my mother, friends, entire families had to perish for the very same reason. I have asked these questions a hundred times, a thousand times, and never received an answer. Nor did I find the time to look for one as I resumed life after the war and tried to forget.

Upon my return from the camps, I went to the United States, where I studied and then worked. In time I was transferred by my employer, IBM, to Europe, where I spent nearly my entire career. I barely allowed myself a moment to search for answers to the questions that haunted me. Retirement provided me that opportunity, but, perhaps subconsciously terrified by the responses that would thrust me back into that world, I put off the research. I still had some old dreams I wanted to realize. My interest in political science, a hobby I have enjoyed for as long as I can remember, was satisfied when I signed up for some courses at Sciences Po, the Institut d'Études Politiques (France's most prestigious school of political science). My life was moving along peacefully. Meanwhile, I kept putting off my ultimate quest.

Then, one ordinary morning, April 8, 1993, my world was shaken. The time had come. In that morning's *International Herald*

Tribune, I discovered an article about a certain Kurt Werner Schaechter that would lead me down a road I knew I had to follow. The title was "Lifting the Veil on Vichy," and beneath it was written: "One Man Tries to Pry Open Archives on French Actions in the Occupation."

Schaechter, a French Jew with Austrian roots, was working diligently to make information available from the period of France's occupation by the Germans. The French archives were not, and still are not, open to the general public. He told Alan Riding, a prominent journalist, about his difficulties. Upon his retirement, Schaechter had begun an investigation to find out what had happened to his parents during the war. He knew they had been deported after being held in Toulouse (in the south of France). Dealing with one bureaucracy after another, he was finally granted special dispensation to consult the archives of the camps in the French region of Haute-Garonne. He was fascinated by the stacks of papers he came across, and among them, he found his mother's identity card. With the help of the young historian volunteering at the archive, he "borrowed" documents in small batches, which he photocopied and returned. Schaechter walked away with more than twelve thousand copies. He felt uncomfortable having to smuggle out this information, but he justified his actions as vital to historical research, since the French authorities had blocked all access to these archives.

This fascinating story plunged me deep into my past. Images resurfaced of my mother, who died in Auschwitz after that terrible "journey" we made together, and of my father, who disappeared very early on and was gassed, and of my own life in hell. This was accompanied by the unrelenting question: How and why did this happen to us? I had to meet Kurt Schaechter. I obtained his address, and a few days later I arrived at his home in the Paris suburb of Alfortville. I spent the entire day listening to his story, poring over the extraordinary documents he had copied. I recall one that was truly shocking, incomprehensible and tragic in its cruel banality: a bill from the SNCF (the French national railway) for the transportation of "prisoners"—one-way fares with the amount in francs per "traveler." Even more extraordinary was the reminder sent, *after* the Liberation, by the SNCF's accounting department to a *préfecture* requesting payment!

That entire day, I was absorbed in the memory of my parents and of what I myself had experienced. It was the spark that pushed me headlong into a desperate search for answers to the questions that were deep in my subconscious. I decided to take action and search the archives for some answers, in spite of the difficulties that Kurt Schaechter warned I might encounter.

As is often the case in these situations, one thing led to another. About a month after I discovered the Schaechter article, my wife called me in to hear a radio program on France-Culture: *Sensitive Archives,* produced by Sonia Combe. As I listened to the guest, Maurice Rajsfus, discuss his research on the Holocaust, I had a strange intuition. My father had disappeared in 1941 after he lost his job. Could he have been one of the Jewish workers transported to the Ardennes region (near the Belgian border) whom they were discussing? I found out how to contact Sonia Combe and, after explaining the reason for my call, asked if I could talk to her guest. She took my number and told me, in a voice full of emotion, that she would give it to him. A few minutes later, the phone rang and Maurice Rajsfus introduced himself. I told him about my intuition and he asked me to hold the line. When he returned, he said these few words that I shall not soon forget: "Your father is in my book." I had for the first time found some trace of him.

That day, the great adventure began. A few weeks later, I traveled with Rajsfus to the town of Bulson in the Ardennes, where my father had lived and worked. There, thanks to stubborn persistence and determination, I found a forgotten box in the attic of the teacher who doubled as the town's mayor and librarian. In it was a list of all the Jews who had worked in that godforsaken, desolate bit of land. My father's name was on the list. We asked the people in the town who were old enough to recall the German Occupation if they remembered "the Jews." I showed a photo of my father, and my heart pounded when I heard one of the men say he thought he recognized the man in the photo as "the man who repaired my shoes." Since that day I have devoted most of my time to reconstructing the past. The result is here for my parents, for myself, and for all those who, like us, believed wholeheartedly that it was possible to be "as happy as God in France."

AS HAPPY AS GOD IN FRANCE

The Gilded Country

My parents, Moshe and Riwka (Riwke, as my father called her) Michlin, had known each other for several years before marrying in 1923 in Niezwiej, a Russo-Polish territory. Life in Niezwiej was difficult. Anti-Semitism made the atmosphere oppressive and they felt the constraints of their religion as well. The young people dreamed of other horizons. Moshe, my father, had studied at the yeshiva and was teaching Hebrew. He dreamed of America, where two of his brothers had settled. One of them, Michael, was ready to welcome Moshe and have him work at the Hebrew school he was running in Detroit. My mother, Riwka, a French teacher, dreamed of living in France where her brother and cousin were living. Her cousin, Mayer Yellin, was working in the garment industry and had set up a cap manufacturing business called Elina. France was, of course, the country of Human Rights. The first country to emancipate the Jewish people, it was a place where they could live well. *Lebn vi Got in Frankraykh,* As Happy as God in France, they would say.

In July 1920, my father took the initial steps to make the move to the United States. At this point, his family had been thrust into a precarious situation, a situation that the following year would become perilous. In a diary my uncle Michael kept in Hebrew, later deciphered for me by my cousin Leah, there is an entry on February 1, 1921. Michael had received letters from my father and my grandparents. A fire had destroyed their house: "They had virtually nothing left to their name." Their departure was imperative. My grandmother asked my uncle to help get two of his brothers started across the Atlantic. My father was going to leave as well. While they waited, Michael sent them some money and had an affidavit issued to my father confirming that he would provide for Moshe financially in the United States if necessary. This official document was essential in order to obtain a visa, but obtaining a visa was not a simple affair. "The shores of the *gilded country* are still very distant," my uncle wrote in his diary three months later. Indeed, so many people dreamed of heading to America that the American consulate in Warsaw had to establish a waiting list. My father would not be eligible until November. Furthermore, the whole enterprise was very uncertain because the visa assured only passage on the ship and not entry into the United States. "The immigration laws," wrote my uncle, "were in the hands of President Harding." At that time, a proposed law was being submitted to Congress to considerably reduce immigrant entrance into the United States by adopting a quota system.

At the end of October 1923, two-and-a-half years after requesting the visa, my father, thanks to the financial support of his brother Michael, was finally able to head to Antwerp, where he boarded the SS *Belgenland* on the Red Star Line. My mother was to join him when he was settled in America. His departure was timely. The perilous situation soon turned tragic. My uncle's diary entry of October 1, 1923, mentions a letter from his brother-in-law that draws a pathetic picture of the situation:

> Our situation is getting worse. We are literally reduced to starvation. We have been hungry for the past three years. This lack of food weakens us little by little, and now it seems our destiny is to live in the most frightful conditions. For three years we have suffered in silence and, not being ones to complain, mentioned nothing of this in our letters. Now we have reached the point where the will to fight has abandoned us. . . . You should know that your sister has only one dress she managed to save from the fire. In fact, she has two

more, but they are not fit to wear as they were sewn together from sacks of Passover flour that were sent to us from America for the Russian refugees.

My father received the visa in time. He arrived in the United States on November 15, 1923. However, he was not permitted to remain. The story is absolutely incredible. I was able to piece it together after a long and detailed analysis and cross-checking thanks to the U.S National Archives and Records Administration and that extraordinary law, the Freedom of Information Act, which allows anybody interested, for personal or family reasons, to consult the National Archives. Such a law in France would certainly be welcome considering that sometimes we are forced, as was Schaechter's case, to find "alternative" means to satisfy the most fundamental right of researching one's family history.

That is how I was able to find "Michlen, Moses" [*sic*] registered on the ship's manifesto as a married man, of Polish nationality, a resident of Nieswiej [*sic*], "race: Hebrew," speaking Russian, able to read and write, and declaring himself to be a teacher. It was definitely my father. He listed as his closest family member my mother, Riwka Michlen [*sic*], born Dworetzki, and his final destination: "Detroit, Michigan." He had only fifteen dollars in his pocket and was neither polygamous nor, in this America rocked by the Sacco and Vanzetti case, an anarchist.

After the first- and second-class passengers got off at Manhattan, the boat headed for Ellis Island, where the third-class immigrants traveling in steerage would be "sorted." I visited Ellis Island, today an historic monument. Try to imagine this little island south of Manhattan accessed by a tourist boat as it passes by the Statue of Liberty, the travelers' first image of America and a promise of happiness that is almost within grasp. An uninviting, brick-colored building awaited the newcomer. My father and his fellow passengers disembarked there. They were directed into a huge lobby leading to a monumental staircase, nearly eighteen feet wide. Everyone had to enter this way. When I visited Ellis Island in 1995, I could not help putting myself in my father's place and reliving what I had experienced when I arrived at the concentration camp. The question of where the stairway led was not to be asked by those taking it. Here, at Ellis Island, as in the camp at Birkenau, people were to move along, without questioning what was going on, without thinking . . . mechanically. It had to be done . . . they did it. Lost in the midst of hundreds of people, they followed like sheep and arrived at the top of the stairs without realizing what was happening: before they took a place on the benches of the great hall on the second floor, immigration officers working for the Department of Labor stood in a passageway above, watching them. They were effecting the initial sorting, the initial "selection." The sick, the lame, the weak and the very old were detected and set aside. Next, a cross would be marked on their clothing with chalk. They were interviewed for good measure, but most of them were sent back. The others were also interviewed, and their responses to the questions would decide their fate. At the end of 1923—the quotas had nearly been filled—only a minority would hear "Welcome to America" and receive the stamp of approval on their visas. It turned out that half of the passengers listed on the manifesto were "deported" (that is the word used on the document). No appeal was possible. My father was one of these passengers. Why?

Officially, my father was rejected because this strong, young man, in good health, who had never been sick a day in his life and would never be sick, had somehow suddenly come down with a "loathsome communicable disease"! After being hospitalized on Ellis Island, set up in a type of quarantine for the illness they had "detected," an illness of which he was completely unaware, my father went before the Board of Special Inquiry on November 22. He was subjected to a pitiful interview. The following is an excerpt from the transcript:

> Alien, sworn, testified through interpreter: A native of Lachowicie; lived for the last three years in Nieswiesk [*sic*], where I have my wife, Rifke.
>
> My brother, Michael, in the US paid my passage; I am a Hebrew teacher. Never in the US before; going to brother at 16250 Delmark Avenue, Detroit, Michigan . . . came to join brother; seek employment and remain permanently. Shows Polish passport issued at Niejsweisk. July 3, 1923, visaed by the American Consul at Warsaw, Poland, July 19, 1923. Born in Pinsk Region. Never debarred or deported.
>
> Q. What provision did you make for the care and support of your wife?
> My wife is also a teacher; she will support herself.
> Q. How long is it since you have seen your wife?
> About two months.
> . . .
> Q. Where did you contract the disease that you have? You are certified with having gonococcus infection of urethra.
> I don't know. Had I known that I had a sickness like that I would not have let it go that far.
> Q. Did you have sexual intercourse with any other woman other than your wife?
> No.
> Q. Tell us the truth. Have you had sexual relations with any woman other than your wife?
> No. I am under oath and I am telling the truth.

Q. Did you have any relations with any woman in a house
  of prostitution or with any woman that you picked up
  on the street?

I swore to it that I am innocent of that.

Q. How do you account for having this disease?

I don't know; for the last two months I have been meeting
  people; on the ship we ate together. I must have contracted it that way.

Q. What you say is physically impossible.

I wish you could read my heart and my soul. I cannot tell
  you anything different than I have because I have told
  you the truth.

Q. There is only one way of contracting the disease and
  that is through a woman who had the disease.

If you want me to swear to it again, I will, for I am telling
  the truth.

Q. Did you have any sexual relations with your wife just
  before leaving for the US?

Yes.

Q. How long before leaving?

About one month.

Q. How long after that did you notice you had the disease?

I was not aware of it and it must be in its first stages for I
  don't feel it.

Q. Do you want this Board to believe that you contracted
  this disease from your wife?

No.

Q. Well then, from whom did you contract it?

I must have contracted it on the ship.

Q. How long has your brother been in this country?

Eleven years.

Q. What is he doing here?

He is a Hebrew teacher.

Q. Have you other relatives here?

Another brother, Mendel, but I don't know where he is living.

After this painful questioning, Inspector Luick moved that the "alien be excluded as being certified by the medical examiners as being afflicted with a loathsome contagious disease, namely gonococcus infection of urethra." The two other board members, Inspector Frayne and President O'Connor, voted with him. Then came the verdict:

> You have been refused admission to the US for the above reason. You have no right of appeal. You will be returned at the expense of the SS company that brought you in the same class that you arrived and without expense to you.

The most staggering part of this tragic story is that a medical certificate was issued that only added to the confusion. The text, the second part of which is incomprehensible, should be appreciated as is:

> Medical certificate nº 5528—11:21/23—This is to certify that the above described person has this day been examined and is found to be afflicted with gonococcus infection of urethra, a loathsome contagious disease. Owing to uncertainty as to alien's condition at the time of embarkation, a statement that the condition herein certified might have been detected by competent medical examination is in our opinion not warranted.

What was the terrible illness my father was suffering from? He was not aware of anything and he "felt nothing." Yet it rendered him very dangerous according to incompetent doctors full of good intentions diagnosing the so-called gonorrhea perhaps as a result of medical knowledge that was still new. Or more likely, could it have been a "political" move, limiting the entrance of immigrants from Eastern Europe—in other words—Jews? In fact, the arrival of my father, who wanted to join his brother Michael in Detroit at the end of 1923, could not have come at a worse time. All the elements seemed to be working against him. In Detroit itself, Henry Ford, the automobile magnate, was ranting against the Jews in his newspaper, *The Dearborn Independent.* In it, he published the infamous czarist fabrication known as *The Protocols of the Elders of Zion.* This anti-Semitic forgery was presented as the minutes of an alleged Jewish conclave convened at the end of the nineteenth century in which Jewish leaders plotted to take over the world. This text, taken at face value, seriously disturbed American legislators, who considered Eastern European Jews the source of a potential revolution. The Immigration Act of 1921 introduced a quota system that was detrimental to Jews of Central and Eastern Europe, and a revision of this law, making it even more restrictive, was in the works during 1923 and would be adopted in 1924 as the National Origins Act.

Of all the places in the world to have as a destination, my father was going to Detroit, a city almost entirely devoted to the automobile—Henry Ford's stronghold. What was he planning to do there? Teach Hebrew, without a doubt. What a tragic and bizarre twist of fate. Fleeing Polish anti-Semitism, he was headed for the American heart of it, and he was soon to encounter it in France and Germany as well. Anti-Semitism was quite probably the reason he was "deported," not the fictitious illness that was claimed. The law was the law and it had to be carried out. Would his fate have been different if he had received his passport earlier and arrived at Ellis Island at the beginning of 1923 when the annual Russian-Polish quota (90 percent Jews) had not been filled? Perhaps. Bad luck certainly played a role. That, rather than the reason my uncle later told me: my father was nearsighted and wore glasses. My uncle believed that was the reason my father was rejected from the United States.

He was mistaken, but he had an excuse. He was a real fan of the Yiddish author Sholem Aleichem, who wrote:

> Where is America? I don't know. I just know that it's far away, terribly far. You must travel and travel for a long time before arriving there. And when you finally arrive, there is a "kestel-gartel" [castle garden] awaiting you. They drop you in the "kestel-gartel," ask you to strip naked and examine your eyes. If you have healthy eyes, it's good news. If not, they make you return to where you came from. It would seem that I have healthy eyes.

But that was not the end of Moshe-Mayer's ordeal. Two of my father's U.S.-born cousins, Morris Cohen, a doctor, and Morris Wainger, an international lawyer (who was later to help me get settled in the United States), wrote to the Commissioner of Immigration to intercede on his behalf. Although they had no access to medical documents, they petitioned:

> Request is hereby made on behalf of above named immigrant, who is destined to his brother at Detroit, Michigan, for leave to remain at Ellis Island Government Hospital, to be cured of ailment from which he is now suffering and which can be cured in several weeks, and for his admission to this country after such cure.
>
> Said immigrant . . . was confined to the hospital suffering from a urethritis, which can be permanently cured by several weeks' persistent treatment. He was ordered deported on account of this condition . . . unless permission is obtained from the Commissioner of Immigration, granting him leave to remain at Ellis Island Hospital to be cured.
>
> A deposit of $165 has been made with the Commissioner at Ellis Island, in accordance with the regulations of this department and in compliance with the request of the authorities at Ellis Island, to pay for the cost of treatment and stay of said patient in the hospital. . . .

The undersigned, therefore, respectfully request that said Moses Michlin be permitted to remain at Ellis Island Hospital until cured, and admitted to this country when cured.

The commissioner would not be moved. The return trip was planned for December 5 or 22. Once again, owing to the work of my father's two cousins who asked for the intervention of a congressman, the case was appealed before a board of revision. The result: "No Hearing." The administration was not about to lose face. They would not accept that this supposed incurable illness could in fact be cured.

The president of the review commission, acting with unusually bad faith as he never asked about the financial situation of the family, drew his own conclusions. He wrote this internal note on December 13 . . . yet another refusal.

This alien is certified to be afflicted with gonococcus infection of the urethra, a loathsome contagious disease. The certificate further shows that because of the chronicity [*sic*] of this disease and its proneness to relapse as well as the possibility of complications, it is impossible to state the length of time required to effect a cure. $165 has been deposited by the alien's Attorney for the first two months hospital treatment, but nothing is shown as to the financial ability of the alien or any relative to continue medical treatment. In view of the fact that this disease cannot be easily cured and the further consideration that the alien is not sufficiently well-fixed financially to warrant the continuing of treatment, it is believed the request should be denied.

Then Frank James, a member of the House of Representatives, received this letter from the Department of Labor dated December 26, 1923, which ended the last hopes of a positive outcome. It was of little importance; my father was already on the boat heading back to Europe:

With reference to your appearance before the Department in behalf of the alien, MOSES MICHLIN, who has been detained at Ellis Island awaiting deportation, I am sorry to be obliged to inform you that the Department can not take favorable action upon the petition for hospital treatment of this young man.

You are aware, I believe, of the fact that this alien has been certified for a loathsome contagious disease, which mandatorily excludes him from admission to the United States. The Immigration Laws provide for the treatment of easily curable diseases, where to effect deportation would work unusual hardship, but neither of these requirements is met by the instant case. The disease for which Mr. Michlin is certified is held by the Public Health Service to be practically incurable, and the length of time required to arrest the disease cannot be estimated. There is not an unusual amount of hardship involved in Mr. Michlin's return, although we must always acknowledge some element of tragedy in every deportation. Mr. Michlin is a young man who has left his wife abroad to whom he may return.

I trust that you are assured of our careful consideration of this case, even though it was not possible to act favorably. The Department can, of course, grant only such relief as is allowed by the provisions of the law which it is administering; and there is no provision for the treatment of a case such as Mr. Michlin's.

Before my father's departure, his brother Michael came to see him on Ellis Island. He wrote this in his diary when he got home: "I spoke to him for an hour. He cried. I tried to control myself. 'Maybe we'll never see each other again,' he said to me."

My father left for Antwerp on the SS *Zeeland* on December 22, passing once more in front of the famous statue, now a cynical allegory of freedom that was refused him.

Returning to Niezwiej in as perfect health as when he left, he wanted to try to get into the United States again by traveling this time in the ship's upper decks using the money his brother had sent him. But an uncle, Shalom Wachsler, discouraged him, as my uncle Michael cites in his diary:

> It would be a terrible thing to attempt to return to the United States, a country where Jews are not welcome. On the other hand, *Eretz Israel* [the Land of Israel] is waiting for young people like you, willing to work.

They considered *Eretz Israel,* but eventually my mother's point of view prevailed; emigration to Palestine was out of the question. Her sister had gone there with her baby, Yasha, to set up a kibbutz (Messilot); it was a harsh existence in the beginning. Her brother Avram (Albert) was in Paris working for their cousin, Mayer Yellin (Elina), in his cap manufacturing company. He had written saying he would be happy to train my father and give him a job. So my father submerged himself in French studies and left once again, this time for France. My uncle Albert was the foreman at the company and welcomed my father with open arms. He trained him as a fabric cutter. After a few days of getting used to his new surroundings, my father began to work in the Elina workshop. Soon my mother joined him.

Living, at Last

I was born on February 5, 1926, exactly nine months after my mother arrived in Paris. The threats of pogroms, along with the *numerus clausus* (discriminatory quota systems), the economic hardship and the religious constraints my parents had known in Poland, were over. Life was beautiful, even carefree. We could barely make ends meet, but we lived with few thoughts for tomorrow and hardly any worries. Here in Paris we were not different from anyone else. Moshe-Mayer became Maurice and Riwka, Renée. And the Russian family name, with a letter that did not exist in French, would be spelled as my uncle spelled his in America, "Michlin." It was pronounced, by chance, like the famous brand of tires.

Both my parents came from large families, but they wanted only one child, as did many French people around them—a child who would go to public school like the other children. They gave me the name Gilbert, or "Gigi" as my mother called me—a real French child's nickname. But I was not simply Gilbert. My mother also called me Zalmonke ("little Solomon"). I was a real little Frenchman and was declared as such when I was born. My father went to city hall to register me as a French citizen according to the law in force. When friends were invited to our house for dinner, I heard Yiddish. But when we were alone, we spoke only French. And what about religion? According to Jewish custom, I was circumcised. But otherwise, I was a real Frenchman—with a different faith but little else to set him apart. Wanting to blend with the majority of people who were secular in France, my parents, who had socialist leanings and read the French newspaper *L'Oeuvre,* adamantly believed in universal values. Although we did not belong to a synagogue, we celebrated Yom Kippur, but we never really fasted. At *Pesach* (Passover), we respected the traditions only slightly more, since it was symbolic of the "deliverance from bondage." I did not even know what *kosher* meant, and I did not become a bar mitzvah when I turned thirteen. There was no *mezuzah* on our door. We led a secular life for the most part.

My parents, officially still foreigners, became good Frenchmen and expected that I would become a true Frenchman as well. However, their desire to integrate into the national community that had welcomed them did not actually wipe out their past and their identity. They socialized with a group that allowed them to maintain connections with a little bit of the world they had left behind. On major Jewish holidays, the few my parents observed, they and their friends from this small community rented a space from the grocers' union on rue du Renard in our neighborhood. The room was turned into a synagogue for the occasion. My father also belonged to a community group (*hevrah kadishah* or holy society), which was very popular among Jewish immigrants. It ensured that all its members could cover the cost of a proper burial. Otherwise, families without money buried their dead in a communal grave. Once a year, we would all go to the cemetery in Bagneux, where my father and other members of the association gathered in front of the headstones in the Jewish section. They would then go to a local café, where everyone would drink schnapps and eat some cake.

My parents sent me to a Jewish boardinghouse in the Paris suburbs every summer. Like most youngsters there, I was bored to tears and could not wait for the week to be over for them to come and visit on the weekend. We often attended the Yiddish-language theater from New York when the troupe was passing through town. Maurice Schwartz and Molly Picon made me laugh so hard with their stories in a Yiddish that I understood, but was not allowed to speak. The stories were written by Sholem Aleichem and were set in the little town of Kasrilevke. It must have resembled my parents' town in Poland. From time to time, we would go out with Jewish friends from the community group. A room was reserved for us on rue Vieille du Temple on the second floor of a modest building. Long tables were set up. All the parents and children ate together. Enthusiastic banter filled the room, and we all enjoyed ourselves thoroughly.

In the very beginning, we lived in the Montmartre section of Paris, between Place Pigalle and Place des Abbesses at 11 rue Véron, with my uncle Albert. My father had lived there since his arrival in Paris. I was only a few months old when, at the end of 1926, we moved to 35 rue Rambuteau. Between Les Halles and the Marais, it was not far from the *Pletzl* (the Jewish quarter of the city) and a few hundred yards from the cap manufacturing company where my father worked. I remember the main entrance at rue Rambuteau perfectly. And I remember Mr. Marcelot who sold poultry there. I also remember his brown-and-white-spotted hunting dog. I remember the fruit and vegetable vendors along the street with their carts on wheels and those fine, long summer evenings when the neighbors would bring their chairs down to the sidewalks and chat endlessly. I also remember the secondhand clothing and rag merchants, Jews for the most part, who shouted to buy or sell *shmattes*. On Sundays, the newspaper vendors sold *L'Humanité* (a communist newspaper) and *L'Action Française* (an extreme right-wing newspaper), facing off and hawking their papers in loud voices. Each week I would buy *Mon camarade,* a weekly periodical for kids, published by the Communist Party. There would be a weekly installment of Mark Twain's *Adventures of Tom Sawyer,* which really appealed to my imagination. I remember the couple who would come down the street singing and selling pamphlets with printed songs, both words and music.

I also remember our small, two-room apartment on the third floor. The entrance was in the back of the courtyard. Our two windows looked onto it. I slept on a sofa, which was in the main room where we ate. It was near the iron potbellied stove whose pipe was attached directly to the chimney. My parents' bedroom was the connecting room. At the back, beyond the bedroom was the kitchen. I remember the gas mantles that provided light in the apartment. We had to ask the concierge, Mrs. Lapostolle, for "the door, please" when we wanted to go out of the building in the evening and announce ourselves when we returned after 10 p.m. And I have memories of the hard white limestone deposit at the bottom of the pot my mother used for boiling water. Concerned about our hygiene and our health, mother always boiled tap water to make it drinkable.

My mother did not work at a paid job; she took care of the house. My father continued to work in the Elina workshops, where he cut piles and piles of material with the aid of a specialized electric saw. The female workers would then sew them together. The cutter was "the aristocrat" of the cap-making profession because the sewers, trimmers, finishers, and pressers depended on his work. He earned a good salary for a top worker in the clothing trade—at that time 340 francs weekly. Our rent was 1,100 francs a year. My mother scrupulously wrote down all of the expenses in a little notebook. We were not rich, but we lived without too much worry by watching our spending.

Sunday was a big day. Uncle Albert often came to the house for lunch. He would prepare the salad dressing, which was made according to a strict ritual—something I enjoyed watching. Along with the oil, vinegar, salt, and pepper, he added a yolk of one or two hardboiled eggs that he would crush with a fork in the vinegar. Then he would cut up the egg white and put it in with the lettuce. The mix was delicious. My mother would prepare a roast chicken for the occasion. In those days, all the chickens had the fresh taste of free-range chickens. The bones were almost edible and we would crunch on them. Without fail my uncle always took the rump of the chicken as I looked on longingly. I was dying to eat that part. It took me twenty-five years before I dared tell him how much he had frustrated me by keeping it for himself. "You should've told me!" came the reply. As if at my age I could have dared to disturb my uncle as he was relishing his favorite part of the chicken.

Apart from Sunday lunches, Uncle Albert did not come to the house. He spent his time at the Café du Commerce on rue des Francs-Bourgeois. I went there from time to time to give him a kiss. After work, he met his friends who, like him, were from Russia or Poland, and they played cards in the smoke-filled room. They did not play just any game of cards; it was always *belote*. It was the only game that could hold their interest, get them excited, and bring silence to the room at crucial moments. It wasn't a good idea to let on that you were giving signals to your partner: *Atout, belote, rebelote, dix de der!* There were several tables of players with four to a table. Spectators surrounded them and looked on with a solemn professional air. They drank tea, glass after glass, and smoked one cigarette after another. At the end of the round, they talked about the game and made running commentaries on the best "plays." They all accused each other of playing poorly. Emotions ran high as they argued in French with some Yiddish words thrown in.

On Sunday afternoons, after my uncle left, I strolled along the Grands Boulevards with my parents. They were similar to what the Avenue des Champs Elysées has become today, but now they are nothing like they were in my day. Theaters, *cafés concerts* (music cafés), and fashionable cafés lined the northern side of the street, and masses of people would stroll along the sidewalks. We would stop at Maxéville, the famous and much-attended *café concert*, where we would listen to the orchestra and singers perform the popular tunes. We often went with friends or met them there. Some Sundays we went to the Gaieté Lyrique, which was on the square between Arts et Métiers and the boulevard Sébastopol. I remember seeing a popular celebrity perform there who really enchanted us— the tenor Willy Tunis in the operetta *Le pays du sourire* (The Land of Smiles). Other times we went to the Comédie Française[1] and saw plays that I had been studying in school. Or we went to the movies on rue Saint-Antoine to see Soviet films like *Tchapaiev* (Chapajev) or *Tarass Boulba* (Taras Bulba). These films were important to my parents because they could see the familiar surroundings of their childhood and, most importantly, hear Russian again. For me, they were superb adventure films. I remember a powerful scene when the hero, using the brute strength of his arms, pumped a platform car's level up and down to move it along the railroad tracks.

And sometimes, on those Sundays, we had lunch at a restaurant with a set menu on rue du Renard. We delighted in a seemingly infinite number of appetizers. When it was very nice out, we went to the Tuileries gardens. My mother would rent a toy boat for me to sail in the pond. We often went to other spots farther away like the Parc de Sceaux, the town of Robinson, and the banks of the Marne.

Sunday mornings, my father, who barely had any free time during the week, took care of me. Sometimes we went to city hall, and I would skate in the open square in front of the building on my skateboard. Or we would go to an even larger square in the courtyard of the Louvre Museum so I could ride my bike. Often, when

---

1. One of the state-subsidized theaters in Paris and the home of French classical drama.

the weather was nice, my father took me to the Deligny swimming pool at the edge of the Seine. I really liked these Sunday mornings. We were on our own, and my father's time was exclusively reserved for me. At these times, he would carefully teach me things like how to swim, ride a bike, and play chess. I remember the advice he gave me if I were faced with an aggressive dog: "If he lunges at you, whatever you do, don't run away. You must remain very still, look him straight in the eye and he won't attack you." Then there was a handkerchief lesson: blowing my nose "one nostril at a time."

Thinking back to those Sunday mornings, I love them all the more. It was the only free time my father had, and he took advantage of it to be with me. The rest of the week, he would leave too early and return in the evening, often too tired to spend time with such a young child. My father was of medium height, slender with dark brown hair that he was losing on the top of his head. He suffered from migraine headaches, and I remember the *calmine* he often took on Saturdays. Although not a regular smoker, he smoked once a week following a completely sacred ritual. He would sit at a table, take out a small box of cigarillos (Ninas), and quietly smoke his cigar of the week. At these times, it was best not to disturb him. Another rite, more frequent than cigar smoking, was drinking tea. It was drunk in two ways: poured into a saucer and sipped directly with a lump of sugar between his teeth (*na prikouski*), which allowed the boiling tea to cool off as it passed through the sugar, or in a cup, sweetened with jam. My father often told me that in Russia, during his youth, he would drink up to forty glasses of tea a day.

When I think back on my father, I remember a strong, healthy man who was very serious and sometimes slightly rigid. I don't recall him laughing. My mother, on the other hand, loved to laugh and laughed often. I still feel close to her. She was very gentle. I remember as clearly as if it were yesterday the time I came down with scarlet fever. I had to remain in a dark room. Instead of going to a literature class she was taking, she spent hours on end, day and night, by my side nursing me back to health. She was there rubbing off the dead skin from my back with cotton and then immediately throwing it in the stove to incinerate the contagious germs.

I liked to watch her taking care of the house and preparing dinner. Of course she made traditional French food, but she also inspired in me a love for Russian-Jewish cooking, with delicious dishes like *borscht, flanken, tschav, tsimmes, gehackte leber, latkes,* and *knaidlach.* When my mother made gefilte fish, it was a real event. I used to go with her to the *Pletzl.* There was a fish store called Klapish facing the school on the rue des Hospitalières-Saint-Gervais, from where so many children were later deported. She would choose a live carp in a tank, and then we would buy some rye bread and other provisions. I enjoyed watching her prepare the carp, in the Russian (Litvak) style—spicy, not sweet in the Polish style. She would gut the fish, stuff it, and put the whole thing in the jelly that was produced when cooking the carp. Then she would add carrots. It was all done according to traditions that were like an art form. Then we would all dig into this gefilte fish, seasoned with a mixture of horseradish and grated beetroot. Much to my disgust, my father would eat the fish head, relishing every bite. "The best part of the carp," he would declare.

While my father taught me to swim and ride a bike, my mother, even before I went to nursery school, taught me to read. With matches, she taught me to count. So when I entered the elementary school on rue de Moussy, I was considerably ahead of the other kids. The teacher, incredulous at my level of reading, tried to stump me by having me read the name of a newspaper: *L'Excelsior.* He was very surprised to hear me read such a complicated word without any difficulty. I skipped a grade immediately. My mother was certainly the one to instill in me a pride in work. She followed my every move. She always encouraged me to work harder and better.

To make her happy, I did everything in my power to be first in the class. There was no greater joy for me than returning from school with the top class medal pinned to my chest.

My mother was intelligent, cultured, and spoke several languages. She was rather small and delicate, with short, light-brown hair and blue eyes. A great beauty, she had an enormous amount of elegance. I remember one day, after saving up her money for quite some time, she purchased one of her long-time dreams—a fox stole. She was in seventh heaven as she modeled her stole wrapped around her neck for us. Unfortunately, several weeks later, she came home from a day out without her precious fox stole. Stolen or lost, we never knew.

Tears come to my eyes when I think back on my mother, my *Yiddishe mama,* who devoted all of her being to ensure that I was in good health and successful. She was always beside me, always discreetly paying attention to what I was doing, never raising her voice, always affectionate. My mother would tell me how she would nurse me when I was an infant four times a day instead of six according to her doctor's wishes, because her milk was too rich and I would soon turn into a blimp if she weren't careful. The lullabies she sang to me when I went to sleep are tunes that I still hum from time to time. Yet, she would tie me to a chair upon her doctor's advice because he feared that I would become bowlegged. And she did not give in to my whims. Once I had been shouting and crying at the top of my lungs for too long. What she did not realize was that I had ended up on the ground with a split eyebrow, and my tears were due to a genuine wound. She also told me how she had to frighten me into taking anti-worm medicine by saying that worms were slithering around in my intestines and if I did not take the medicine, they would carry me off, asleep, to the Seine river, only a few hundred yards from our house. Even today, her presence is with me when I walk through certain neighborhoods, certain streets and gardens in Paris.

My parents welcomed friends to the house often. They were not my father's colleagues, because he tended to keep his work and social life separate. They were the parents of my friends or friends from the association to which my parents belonged. Sometimes friends from Russia would visit. I remember Mr. Grazovsky. He fascinated me because he had no teeth. I watched in amazement as he would cut an apple into slender sections and then proceed to gum them down.

I must not neglect to speak of the books that were brimming over on our bookshelves. Of course, the book awards for excellence and honors that I received each year were placed there (Jules Verne, Erkmann-Chatrian), but also many other books bought over the years that my mother and I would read voraciously (Grimm's Fairy Tales, Hans Christian Andersen, Honoré de Balzac, Victor Hugo, Alexandre Dumas).

Even though we were happy, I had a few regrets about our modest income. Some of the things so familiar in homes today were considered useless luxuries then. We did not have them. We never had a radio, and I sometimes envied my classmates who would talk during recess about the adventures of the Duraton family from a popular program, which I had to experience vicariously. I never went to the seashore either, but I did not miss it. What I knew about it, I heard from my schoolmates who talked about their vacations or from pictures of my uncle wearing a bathing suit on some beach on the Riviera.

Around the time of my tenth birthday, we moved a bit farther away to the rue Geoffroy l'Angevin, at number 2. We had a two-room apartment on the fourth floor of a six-story building. As in rue

Rambuteau, I slept on the sofa in the main room. The table on which we ate our meals and around which friends would gather was the same and located in the same place, while my parents' bedroom was in the next room. On the wall in the main room was a beautiful tapestry of Pompeii that my mother had brought with her from Russia. The kitchen was more practical than the one on rue Rambuteau, and the Turkish toilet (a water-flushed bowl on the ground with no seat) was on the small landing between two floors. In all, it was about 325 square feet with three windows looking onto the street.

My friends were the same after our move. Félix Russac was my competition for first place in the class. I liked playing with him in the basement of the building where he lived. In that awesome, but unsettling vaulted cellar, we liked to give each other a scare. With the strong scent of saltpeter in the air, we would light candles and pretend to be ghostly figures. There was also my oldest friend Jacques Birenbaum, "Jacquot," whom I had known since nursery school. Our school was on the Beaubourg plateau where the whimsical fountain by Niki de Saint-Phalle and Tinguely is today. There were public schools for various ages—a nursery school, a girls' elementary school on rue Brise Miche, and a boys' elementary school on rue Saint-Merri. Jacquot's parents lived on rue Brise Miche, just opposite the nursery school. My mother would come and wait for me after school and talk to Jacquot's mother. They became friendly. His parents ran a small business making leather jackets, which meant they had more money than we did. The surest sign of that was that their toilet was in their apartment and not on the landing like ours. I remember the toilet's door covered with holes from darts; we often missed the target hanging on the door. These friendships still continue to this day. After my return from the camps and after having lived in the United States, I looked up Jacquot and Félix and renewed our friendships. Félix died a few years ago of a stroke.

On rue Geoffroy l'Angevin, I made another friend, Maurice Culet. His parents owned the Hôtel d'Annecy opposite our apartment. We saw each other often and did our homework together. We would jog together on the Beaubourg plateau, which was then just an open area, showing little of the promise of today's Pompidou Center. In those days, we had Thursdays off from school in France. Maurice and I would go to the Cinéac movie theater on the rue de Rivoli in the afternoon. I found a way to see two different films for the price of one ticket. If you went in on Thursday afternoon at a certain time, you could take advantage of the transition of the movie program from one week to the next. We had great fun watching the antics of Charlie Chaplin, the Marx Brothers, and Laurel and Hardy.

Maurice was a great friend. A few months before our arrest in 1944, my mother had a strong premonition of the danger we were in. She asked Maurice's parents if they would keep a little suitcase filled with our important documents in their country house in Saint-Maur. She filled it with my papers, my awards, our diplomas, photographs, my parents' passports, their *ketubbah* (marriage contract) and other important documents. When I got out of the camps after the war, I went to pick up the precious suitcase. I remember being ecstatically grateful to Maurice's parents for having kept these treasures. However, later on when I thought it over, I radically changed my point of view. I was slightly disgusted. Why this drastic change? I remember those days when the dread was horrible for us, the roundups were more frequent, and people were disappearing. My mother felt that something terrible was going to happen. I think back to her, in the country house where we went to drop off the suitcase, and I am certain today that she was secretly hoping that my friend's parents would offer to hide us there. But silenced by pride and not wanting to trouble them, she did not say anything. Yet it would have been easy for them to keep us in this isolated suburb. They did not have the presence of mind to make the offer, which would have doubtless saved her life.

Since I began writing about my experiences, I have thought back to that scene often. Maurice's mother understood that my mother was in dire straits. The very fact of bringing the suitcase was proof of it. The risk of hiding my mother in this house was virtually nonexistent. Maurice's mother preferred not to take any risk. Our problems were not hers, and perhaps her anti-Semitism was the real reason. I remember she later talked to my wife about my mother, giving her a compliment, "Your mother-in-law was Jewish, but she was *clean.*"

In the end, was Maurice's mother different from anybody else? The French people who saved the Jews were few in number, whatever attempts have been made to prove the contrary. Some Jews of the establishment try to smooth over the situation by spouting elegant phrases and telling the French what they want to hear. But the facts are all there, researched and exhibited at the very source—Yad Vashem.[2] After more than half a century of painstaking research, there have been only twenty-one hundred French people declared "Righteous," worthy of recognition for having saved Jews during the war. At best, they saved twenty thousand Jews, a very small number compared to the estimated three hundred thousand Jews living in France at that time. The Jews who were able to escape being arrested more often than not had to get by on their own. There were certainly some heroes whose stories will be left untold. However, often the help that people offered was not free of charge. How many people took advantage of distressed families to earn a

---

2. A museum and memorial in Jerusalem dedicated to victims of the Holocaust. It also honors resistance fighters and "Righteous Gentiles" who helped Jews during World War II.

little extra cash, not to mention the Catholic Church, which did hide Jewish children, but much too often at the price of "conversion." Jewish parents accepted these terms out of desperation.

The general French population was at best completely indifferent to the Jews' plight and remained that way, following the example of the various governments, left wing and right wing, that came to power after the Liberation. It was not until 1995 that President Jacques Chirac allowed France to face its painful past and recognize its collaboration in the persecution and deportation of the Jews. Better late than never, as the saying goes. But having to wait for over fifty years . . .

After finishing elementary school, at eleven years old, with my diploma with honors in my pocket, I graduated to an intermediate school on rue Montgolfier, just behind Ecole Centrale. Because I had skipped some grades, I was too young to compete for entrance to the Dorian technical school. I had to be "patient," and wait until I was old enough to apply for this school, as my father wished. My mother wanted me to be a doctor, but my father was adamant on the issue. I must "learn a manual skill." His personal experience as an intellectual who could only teach Hebrew certainly played a major part in his decision. His viewpoint was confirmed in the Talmud: "a blessing upon a man who works with his hands." And of course a manual skill offers the advantage of being able to "transport" it with you, having it "in hant" (at hand). I would therefore not be able to go to a French "Ivy League" school or any university, no matter how good my grades were. I was to apply to the technical school, and having done well on the competitive entrance exam, I became a tool-and-die maker. At the school on rue de Moussy, I really appreciated the shop classes that were part of the general curriculum. We worked with wood and iron, putting objects together, and I would proudly bring them home. It was a real pleasure for me. But to base my entire career on this was another matter.

In contrast to my parents' plans for me, I had other dreams. My heart was set on becoming an actor. Beginning in nursery school, I would look for any occasion to act in plays. When we had dinner at the home of friends, I would get the other kids to put on a play for the parents. In school, I always acted in plays, even performing all the roles, like the time I was the servant and the *bourgeois gentilhomme* in Molière's play for my teacher and schoolmates. The performance earned me long applause. And when my mother took me to the Comédie Française, I was fascinated and marveled at how the actors could change roles every day and perform something new from their extensive repertory. I really saw myself as an actor, but I could not see myself acting the same role every night. That left only the Comédie Française or the cinema.

When I was at school, even though I took my studies very seriously, I loved making my classmates laugh. One of my favorite acts was pretending to pass a needle and thread into my ear and through my head to the opposite ear, or I would throw an imaginary ball up to the ceiling. I would follow its trajectory with my eyes and catch it when the teacher turned to the blackboard. The class would burst into fits of laughter; the teacher would turn around and I would be sitting there impassively. My report cards reflected the consequences of these actions in the column under behavior in class. Later on, during the German Occupation, I learned that Charles Dullin, the prominent actor and director, was giving classes in the Théâtre de la Cité (formerly the Sarah Bernhardt Theater, whose name has never been restored). I discreetly found a way to attend his classes from time to time, though it was officially off limits to Jews. That way, I was able to get close to acting, though I never got to satisfy my dream.

I was never to be an actor, but rather a die maker. And when I was taking classes at the intermediate school, so was my friend Félix Russac. I also met two new friends, Maxime Doukhan, the son of the concierge of the Palais de Justice, and Henri Tchervinsky, the son of a jeweler on rue Rambuteau. Once I completed classes at the intermediate school, I was able to take the competitive exam and entered Dorian technical school.

My specialization in aeronautics demanded a lot of work. I no longer had Thursdays off, and that meant no more movies. I worked twice as hard, having to attend both professional classes and the regular curriculum, all from 8 a.m. to 6 p.m. every weekday and Saturday morning as well. What's more, Dorian was located quite far from our home, so I had to get up at 6 each morning to be at school by 8 a.m. And when I got home, I did my homework until 2 a.m.

It was around this time that I began to realize that being Jewish was not only being like everybody else with just some differences in traditions, holidays, and cooking. I also realized that being Jewish was, for some unexplainable reason, something that did not appeal to everybody. Yet these disapproving people, as far as I could see, were not very different from us. I remember the slogans I read everywhere, such as "France for the French." These offensive attacks and putdowns came from people like our neighbors whom we called *cagoulards* (members of a secret extreme right-wing group). I never understood why these neighbors living on the floor below us, who owned a little restaurant in the building, seemed to hold a grudge because we walked over their heads. And without really understanding it all, I chose my camp. How many times during recess did my friends and I fight with the "fascist" kids, who were conscientiously developing opinions they heard from their parents, members of the Croix de Feu and PSF (extreme right-wing groups). Sometimes I was frightened. On the night of February 6, 1934, violent right-wing demonstrations erupted over the Stavisky affair, a financial and political scandal that began with a Jewish bond seller and swindler and shook the country. I was overcome with anxiety as my mother grew worried because my father did not return home from work at his usual time.

Anti-Semitism was widespread. My parents were sensitive to the negative repercussions of the Stavisky affair. One Jew cannot be a swindler without all Jews taking the blame. My parents' feelings were divided between elation and fear at the victory of the Front Populaire (the Popular Front political party) and the nomination of Léon Blum, a Jew, to the position of premier. They were concerned that it might incite more hatred. Bold headlines invariably pinned everything bad on the Jews and filled my parents with apprehension. Newspapers were not the only negative medium. I remember my parents' anger, a resigned anger that came from constantly dealing with the Catholic Church's hatred, which they thought they had escaped. The mystery play *Vray Mistère de la Passion* (True Mystery of the Passion), written by Arnould Gréban in the fifteenth century, was put on every year for at least one week in the square in front of Notre Dame Cathedral. With more than a thousand participants and thousands of spectators, it was a big event. The play portrayed all the Catholic anti-Jewish thought. Its point of departure was the fact that too few Jews deigned to convert to Christianity in spite of the threats, exactions, expulsions, killings, massacres, and various inquisitions. Under the patronage of the Church, on the square in front of Notre Dame, they would speak of Jews as "traitors," "guilty," "perverse and envious," and "deceitful dogs."

Of No Interest to the Nation

In 1933, my father undertook the necessary steps to acquire French citizenship. He gathered the required documents and waited patiently to be invited to an interview. He had to wait until 1936. A police investigation had established his character, morality, and conduct: "good"; his revenues and financial situation: "mediocre"; his "attitude with regard to the present government": "correct" and "favorable." Then they tried to discern if he was ready to "renounce any and all desire to return to his country," if he lived "in a milieu that was exclusively French," and if he sought out "friends among foreigners or French nationals." With so many unanswered questions, he was finally called to meet with the police chief in the Saint-Merri police precinct. This was clear from the papers I was able to consult through a special dispensation on "an extremely exceptional basis" after a long series of correspondence exchanged with the various ministries over fifteen months. My father was called to a formal interview in 1936 to update information gathered by police investigators and to answer various other questions. One of their concerns was whether he was prepared to pay the 1,276 francs fee for naturalization and 675 francs for "reintegration"; they also questioned the exact motive behind his request. Regarding the fees, he responded in the negative, offering as the law in force permitted, a sum corresponding to his resources: 300 francs. As to his motive, he responded by "claiming the rights and privileges accorded to all French citizens," a response which was in complete accordance with the Declaration of Human Rights. Other questions were also asked: "Did he serve France during the war?": "No." "Did he have a French diploma?":

"No." But the "petitioner is in good health and knows how to read, write and speak our language fluently." After this interview in 1936, the decision dated October 12, 1933, was not modified; the police chief of the Saint-Merri precinct remained absolute:

> With respect to the main request, as well as to the possible reduction of State fees to be paid for naturalization, the present request holds no interest to the nation. The possible reduction in State fees is without merit.

Why was my parents' naturalization request of "no interest to the nation?" Was it because they weren't wealthy, or was it because they were Jewish? Apart from religion, which was of little interest to them, what was the difference between my parents and the typical French national? They were literate, extremely so. Along with French, they spoke and wrote Polish, Russian, and other languages. They were not anarchists. They loved France more than the average Frenchman. Having lived in another culture, they had a point of reference and could appreciate France all the more. The administrative hierarchy probably had not changed between 1933 and the arrival to power of the Front Populaire in 1936 . . . as it would barely change at the Liberation after the German Occupation.

"The qualifications of the foreigner are insufficient," the police *préfet* concluded, and his "interest to the nation" as well, declared the minister. The request (Central Record no. 901090) was adjourned for three years. My father received only a letter dated June 2, 1939, advising him of the three-year adjournment; no reason was given. He could re-present his case in 1942. For obvious reasons, he was not able to do so.

For the first time in the summer of 1938, my parents did not send me to one of those boardinghouses where I was bored to death.

Instead, with my friend Jacquot, they sent me to the country to live with a family in Bouray-sur-Juine, a few miles from Arpajon (about thirty-five miles south of Paris). We stayed in a *café-hôtel* near the railroad tracks. Every day, when we weren't chasing a few pretty girls in the area, we would watch the trains go by. In the evening, we would sit down to a meal with everyone present. We avoided eating the *chabrot* (an unusual soup to which wine was added with bits of bread floating in it) that our hosts adored, but we would listen to their conversations. They talked about the Germans, the imminence of war, and the invincibility of France. The Germans could try to attack us, but we weren't in any danger, they said. We had the best army in the world, the best soldiers and the best generals, the best weapons, and a Maginot Line where they would knock off all the Hitlers of the world. What's more, we had a secret weapon. Systems had been installed in the interior of the renowned Maginot Line, which would use high-powered rays to stop the enemy planes' engines. The Germans would certainly be surprised when they tried to invade and saw their planes plunge uncontrollably to the ground. Jacquot and I were only twelve, but we were amazed at these gullible adults who exhibited such blind confidence. How could adults believe such nonsense? But they were certain that these were absolute truths. How could anyone accept facts at face value without exercising the slightest critical analysis? I still often wonder about it now.

The threat of Germany and its growing army was felt across all of Europe. Yet it only seemed a distant menace for me. I was certainly not totally blinded by France's secret rays. My demanding work at technical school took up most of my time and energy. When there was a break from these studies, I wanted to do only one thing. I would get on my bike and go with Maurice Culet to his house in Saint-Maur. Sundays were tiring because I had to keep up with Maurice on his racing bike.

Two events stand out in my mind from this time: the 1937 World's Fair, which took place in Paris, and the Soviet-German pact in 1939. The German and Soviet pavilions at the fair faced each other. The Soviet pavilion featured a male and female couple made of stone, carrying a hammer and sickle. As if mutually defying each other, they stood opposite a huge German eagle set on a swastika. This made a profound impression on me. When the Soviet foreign minister Molotov and the German foreign minister Ribbentrop signed that well-known pact in 1939, it was wrenching for my parents, who greeted it with total incomprehension. How could the USSR give free reign to the Nazi Germans by allowing them to make war in the West in the hope that the Soviets would be spared? I heard such conversations in our home, and I felt a great nervousness rising in my parents. And what about the Munich agreement, the preceding year? That great sigh of relief was just a deceptive move by the Germans. The elite running the French government was cowardly, bending to popular opinion.

A question would arise when we talked of war that seemed more and more inevitable every day. What would my father do? This question really made me anxious. And when, in 1939, war was declared, I was proud to see my father, a foreigner, immediately volunteer with a group of his friends as part of an association of Jewish volunteers. But he was not enlisted, undoubtedly owing to his age (42) and his terrible nearsightedness.

Then came the "Phony War." Everybody was waiting around at the front stagnating, and nothing much was happening. Terse military communiqués were sent: "nothing to report." The fear of the unknown was dissipating and confidence was on the rise. It was clear that the Germans were afraid of the French, who would win the day "because we were the strongest" and we would "hang our laundry out on the Siegfried Line"[1] . . . as the soothing slogans ran.

---

1. Germany's counterpart to France's Maginot Line.

At this point, I was still pursuing my intense studies at Dorian, where all my courses were interesting, particularly mathematics. Ever since my discovery of algebra a few years earlier, it always held a fascination for me. I tried to apply myself as best as I could to the manual tasks. I did not much like them, but I had to persist. My father had impressed that lesson upon me clearly. I learned how to do everything: read a blueprint, level off a metal surface with a file so that it was set straight against backlighting. The work gave me blisters on the palm of my right hand. I learned to sharpen a drill so that it would bore perfectly at the punch mark, how to lathe, mill and rectify, and using India ink, how to draw the front, side, and upper views of a complicated piece of machinery on transparency so that it could be made with the appropriate tolerance.

And then, suddenly, like a flash of lightning in a bright blue sky, on May 10, 1940, the blitzkrieg began. The German army attacked with endless rows of tanks advancing on France. They bypassed the Maginot Line, which proved useless. The French army was in full flight and in great disarray. It seemed unable to put up any resistance. The people in the north of France began to flee their cities and villages, taking refuge farther south.

Then the Parisian population began to flee. This exodus provoked a veritable panic in me. I saw all my friends and neighbors escaping. Choking down the tears, I told my parents that after all we had heard about the Germans, we could not possibly stay. We were aware of their ideas about Jews and what was going on in Germany, how much they wanted to hurt them, hurt us. How could we even consider staying? And I saw people who were not Jewish, who had even less to fear than we did, escaping. We had to follow them. I pleaded with my parents. I cried inconsolable tears and could not understand why they were so set on staying. But where would we go, and what would we do without money? They did not want to traipse around as they had done several years earlier when they tried to go to the United States and then France. Maybe my parents were right. We stayed. France was soon defeated. I remember the arrival of the Germans in Paris on June 14, 1940. That date remains indelibly engraved in my memory, like others soon to come. That was the day I understood that money could often be the means of attaining freedom.

I remember going to the square in front of city hall. German flags with swastikas replaced the French flag. The green German uniform began to crop up everywhere, and even when we looked up into the sky we saw Germany again with the little black plane that would fly around in circles. France had capitulated. The country had been brought to its knees and requested an armistice. WHAT A CALAMITY.

It was a shock, a genuine shock after all that had been said about the Maginot Line, our incomparable strength, and our invincible army. People were saying that our leaders were on the run. All their great claims turned out to be illusions.

And then . . . life took up as before. The Germans were extremely friendly, polite, and helpful. They would carry heavy bags for women and give up their seats to ladies on the subway. "Maybe they are not as monstrous as we heard," people were beginning to say. There must be a way to work things out.

Toward the end of 1940, after the partial occupation of France by Germany, Hitler wanted to emphasize his consideration for France and for Marshal Pétain (chief of state of the Vichy government), who, in October 1940, had already demonstrated his eagerness to cooperate by having his government implement a special statute regarding Jews. Hitler shook hands with Pétain and thus sealed the new political collaboration with Germany. As a further reward, Hitler ordered that the ashes of the King of Rome, Duke of Reichstadt, son of Napoleon and Marie-Louise, be returned to Paris. In the name of a "grateful" France, Admiral Darlan welcomed the coffin at the Dôme of the Invalides in Paris, which contains Napoleon's remains, and the religious ceremony was presided over by Cardinal Suhard, Archbishop of Paris.

Soon after this, I realized that my parents had been right not to leave Paris because everybody who had left, returned. This reassured me.

I continued my studies. My uncle Albert, who had been drafted, was taken as a prisoner of war. And my father was absolutely desperate. He had lost his job. Mayer Elina, with admirable foresight, had closed down his company in June 1940. It reopened a few months later headed by one of his non-Jewish friends. This gave him the chance to liquidate the company's inventory, a shrewd move on his part anticipating the Aryanization of businesses by the French general commissioner in charge of the Jewish Question, which was a part of the Vichy government.

My father was unable to find work as a fabric cutter for caps in another company, so he decided to change his profession. He began to work as a waiter in a restaurant, while learning to make buttonholes manually, hoping a tailor would hire him. I do not know if this skill would have allowed him to find another job, but soon after that he left for the Landes region in southwest France to work as a lumberjack. This was the result of an action taken by the Labor Ministry through the commissioner on unemployment, all part of the Vichy government.

The only thing I remember is that my father disappeared from the house, and I never knew where he had gone. My mother never mentioned it. When did he leave? I don't know. I was able to piece together what happened to my father by consulting various archives. He must have left in the spring of 1941 because when the Vichy government law of June 2, 1941, demanded that a census of all Jews be taken, my father was no longer there. I remember going to sign up for the "census" with my mother next to the Louvre

Museum on rue Bailleul where the police *préfecture* had set up an annex. After a long wait, we were registered. We remained upstanding citizens. France demanded it, and so we were able to avoid "imprisonment of one month to one year and a fine from 100 to 100,000 francs, or one of these sentences not withstanding the right of the prefect to decide upon the internment in a special camp, *even if the concerned party is French.*"

In Landes, my father joined a group of lumberjacks. Some of them were Jewish men who, like him, had been recruited by "the unemployment office." This camp was located in Belin-Joué, about twenty-five miles south of Bordeaux. My father and his fellow workers were in charge of clearing the ground, establishing cycling trails, and setting up forest routes. A foreman headed up a group of 250 workers. They lived in barracks that held fifty of them and could be dismantled.

At some point, the Germans discovered there were Jews on the work site, which was very near the Atlantic Wall constructed by the German organization Todt to prevent any Allied landing. On December 24, 1941, gendarmes arrested my father and escorted him and twenty-one others to the foreigners' section of the internment camp (officially called "assigned residence") at Mérignac-Beaudésert, not far from Bordeaux.

At that time, the French state had recently created L'Union Générale des Israélites de France (UGIF, the French Union of Israelites in France), to group together all the old Jewish cultural, philanthropic, and social institutions. UGIF was attempting to fulfill its role as well as it could, believing with disarming good faith, that they could do something to improve the plight of Jews in France. Taking up Pétain's agricultural propaganda, it had just set into motion a project to "return to the land." Georges Bloch, one of UGIF's executives, had signed the following appeal, which I was able to find in New York at the YIVO Institute for Jewish Research, the pre-eminent center for the study of Eastern European Jewry and Yiddish. This appeal shows the full extent of the UGIF directors' naïveté.

Jews and agriculture

One of the main complaints against Jews, if not the main one, is that they are unfit to work the land. If we all join together to prove that the people of our faith can adapt to this type of labor, we are certain that the Jewish question might evolve in a completely different manner in France. We are happy to let you know that the question is now, for our part, resolved. The authorities on which we depend are aware of our project and have decided to help us with all the means available to them. We are now ready to begin sending single Jewish men between the ages of 18 and 45 who desire to make a living or change profession in accordance with the French government's statutes regarding Jews that have been imposed upon us, by working with French farmers. We already have a placement service in liaison with official organizations and we can now handle the placement of men who truly want to work. It is now up to you to collaborate with us. It is now essential that all those who feel able to work in the following capacities: farmhand, carter, ox herder, shepherd, etc., should come join our ranks.

We have done our duty; now it is up to you to do yours. If you want to preserve the presence of the Jewish population in France, we must prove that we are able to face up to these grievances against us. We are counting on you to come and sign up. You must join us in great number because our salvation now depends on you.

That is how, having received very little success by voluntary conscription, the UGIF focused on the internment camps to recruit single men and married men as well. Ostland, a German company, was looking for extra manpower to work in the Ardennes region. The UGIF went to the camps. They were well aware that working conditions were difficult in the Ardennes region—winters were bitter cold, housing was underequipped and not adapted to the harsh conditions, and salaries were ridiculous, much lower than for non-Jewish workers. There was a virtual absence of doctors, and food was insufficient and of poor quality. In its internal correspondence, the UGIF often made references to the complaints of the workers. But as Bloch had written, the "Jewish question," thanks to the agricultural work, "had to evolve in a entirely different manner in France." The representatives of the UGIF continued to recruit people by holding out the prospect of better living and working conditions than in the camps and by guaranteeing the protection of the families that remained at home. On January 26, 1942, the UGIF wrote to the prefect of the Gironde region, trying to obtain the "pure and simple" liberation of the twenty-two prisoners from Mérignac. Realizing the gendarmes would never approve, the letter asked the prefect, as a last resort, to permit the prisoners to be transferred to the Ardennes region so they could work for Ostland. In its letter, the UGIF advised that the Germans were in agreement with the project. The sender of the letter added that "the 22 inmates" would "enthusiastically welcome this transfer." It took place on March 18, 1942. The gendarmes, required by the prefect "in the name of the French people," according to laws dated July 19 and August 3, 1791 (!) and to decrees dated October 4, 1891, and May 20, 1903 (!), escorted the prisoners from Mérignac to Paris. They were to be transferred to the Ardennes region the following week. My father was one of these men. He arrived on March 27 in Bulson, a desolate place some eighteen miles from Charleville-Mézières, a French territory close to the Belgian border exclusively under German control, with some UGIF delegates stationed there.

I don't know exactly what my father's life was like there, until January 5, 1944, when he was arrested along with the other Jews in Ardennes to be deported to Auschwitz via the Drancy internment camp. Various correspondences found in papers from the UGIF at YIVO can give us a broad idea of the fears and terrors my father and his companions might have experienced. Here is a terrible letter that was addressed to the UGIF from a distraught worker at Bulson:

Bulson, September 28, 1942

Sir,

We have learned here with great emotion that a list of 36 children of the Ardennes workers who were to be liberated have arrived at the Drancy camp and that among these 36 children, only two could be liberated. The others have already departed for nobody knows where.

My wife and my two children, ages 6 and 4, were interned at Beaune-la-Rolande. Perhaps, might it be possible, that at least the children be liberated even if unfortunately the mother is not.

I am writing this to you as a father, Sir, and am sure you will understand my insistence in this matter. I beg of you to make your best efforts in favor of my children, and if possible, my wife.

Thank you in advance for whatever help you can offer in this situation.

Sincerely yours,

Binstejn, Elie, in Bulson par Haraucourt (Ardennes)

In Paris, 12, rue des Cendriers 20th arrondissement

The workers in Ardennes were theoretically protected up to a certain point. The Germans had made an "agreement" with the UGIF to protect the workers' belongings and protect their families from being arrested. The UGIF often had to intervene to stop eager French initiatives against those families as well. But naturally the power of the UGIF was illusory, and the German promises were without commitment on their part. The directors of the UGIF were quickly aware of this situation, but continued on as if nothing were wrong, whatever the consequences. They continued their work, scrupulously maintaining in their books a detailed list of the women and children of the husbands working in Ardennes, along with their complete addresses in order to "assure" a pseudo-protection. For people like Elie Binstejn, this "protection" could be withdrawn at any time, as it was invariably withdrawn in our case when my father was arrested.

The directors of the UGIF were naturally fully aware of the cause-and-effect relationship between the arrest of my father and all of his friends in Ardennes and the suspension of the "protection" of their families. Between my father's arrest on January 5, 1944, and our arrest, four weeks went by, certainly sufficient time for the UGIF to warn us of the imminent danger hanging over our heads. The UGIF chose to let the French police conscientiously carry out their job, making sure that the railroad cars of convoy number 68 were tightly packed on February 10, 1944. Perhaps the UGIF, for "humanitarian reasons," was interested in "family reunions."

To illustrate the "total confusion" of the UGIF, one must read another letter, an indirect response to the letter on the previous page. It provides information as to the plight of the children arrested and sent to Drancy, a transit camp that was under the administration of the French *préfecture de police.* It was signed by one of the UGIF executives, Israelowicz, a Viennese Jew who had been imposed by Theodor Dannecker, the SS officer heading the *Judenreferat,* a special police branch for Jewish questions. The letter is addressed to Eszkenasy, a delegate of the UGIF in Ardennes:

October 15, 1942
Sir,
With reference to the conversations we had and your letter of

October 8, I have the pleasure to bring the following information to your attention:

Our first request concerning the protection of the women and children of the agricultural workers in the Ardennes region was not taken into consideration by the German authorities. However, a second attempt on August 24 resulted in the creation of a list of 34 children who were to be freed from the camp.

As we customarily do, we sent the liberation order of August 25 from the German police to the Préfecture de Police. It was clear for us that the children on the list would be liberated. After a few days, not having heard anything on the subject of the liberation of the children in question, we made a request to the Préfecture and learned to our great dread that the list had been lost. After much difficulty, we obtained on September 15 that the list be signed a second time. Unfortunately, most of the children that were to be liberated had already been deported.

I don't need to tell you how much this state of affairs is regrettable for us. From the description that precedes, the circumstances show clearly that it is difficult to find the person responsible for this situation.

Then a few sentences at the end express satisfaction that the apartments of the workers in Ardennes were protected. Unconsciousness aligned with disgraceful actions! On the one hand, the UGIF had the "pleasure" of informing them that the "major" part of thirty-four children who should have been liberated were in reality deported, and on the other hand, the *préfecture de police* had "lost" the list of the children. In fact, the *préfecture* was perfectly aware, as they were the ones to give the order, that the police had transported four thousand children *without parents* a few weeks earlier, in buses that would drop them off at the Drancy camp. This was the final step before deportation, which would take place on August 17, 1942 (convoy number 20 and the following convoys).

Barely one year later, my father and his companions were arrested and transferred to Drancy. From there, on January 20,

1944, they left for Auschwitz. We know, thanks to the work of Serge Klarsfeld, that an investigation should have been initiated and undertaken by the *préfecture de police* as to what happened to those who departed that day. From convoy number 66, which carried 632 men and 515 women, there were only forty-five survivors. My father was not one of them. He was gassed upon arrival, because of the glasses he wore to correct his nearsightedness. The notorious doctor Josef Mengele, who presided over the arrivals at Birkenau, considered it a sign of an unforgivable infirmity.

In 1941, I was still a hardworking student, but not unaware of the events going on around me. In fact, since the June 1940 armistice, an oppressive atmosphere had settled in and seemed to be getting worse. Pétain's government, in symbiosis with the German occupiers, was quick to sign anti-Semitic laws in keeping with the National Revolution, anticipating the Germans' desires. These measures, not applicable to the rest of the population, left non-Jews generally indifferent. Life in Paris continued. People went to the movies, theaters, and restaurants, and the café terraces were overflowing with people. The success of the PMU (off-track betting) continued. A non-Jewish friend of my uncle Albert worked there and told us all about the exciting horse races. But for most Parisians, life was very difficult because food was rationed. You had to run to different places to get any food, and this was done after a long day of exhausting work and endless commuting.

This general attitude of indifference prevailed as a series of French laws and German rulings relegated all the Jews—French and foreigners—to the ranks of second-class citizens, from both a social and a professional standpoint. In the meantime, Jews were asked to register as such and wear a distinctive mark—a yellow star. This policy of exclusion from public life and the French economy pushed the Jews into unemployment. It played into the hands of those ready to accuse the Jews of all evils, including parasitism. Like my father's experience at Ellis Island, every Jew suddenly seemed to be afflicted with a *loathsome communicable disease.* And as at Ellis Island, no appeal was possible. If you had three Jewish grandparents you were persecuted, or if your spouse was Jewish, only two Jewish grandparents were enough.

In May 1941, we learned that hundreds of Jews—foreigners, for the most part—were called to the police stations. They confidently went, but did not return. They were sent to internment camps in Loiret province at Pithiviers and Beaune-la-Rolande. A collective psychosis was taking hold of the Jewish families in Paris that would get worse a few months later. In August, a rumor got out that roundups were taking place at subway exits in the 11th arrondissement. People were saying that only men were being arrested. Even though my father was no longer in Paris, my mother was very apprehensive. She tried to hide it from me.

I continued my studies without respite as my mother encouraged me even more fervently to get the best grades in all my subjects. Caught up in my work, and accustomed to the repeated absences of my father, sometimes for protracted periods owing to the variety of precarious jobs he took on, I did not notice his permanent absence right away.

On June 22, 1941, the French press blared the headlines that Germany had begun an extensive attack against "bolshevism." Nothing could stem the tide of this lightning war. German tanks were barreling across miles and miles of territory. The Soviet Red Army was retreating. The invincibility of the German army knew no bounds. The Légion des Volontaires Français (LVF, Legion of

French Volunteers) against bolshevism was created to restore the glory to France that the country sorely needed. France would fight alongside the victorious German army.

My mother already sensed the beginning of the end. She thought back to Napoleon and his army's rout across the Berezina River in 1812, and she tried to give me hope by reciting to me passages from Pushkin in Russian that could apply to Hitler and his gang. Meanwhile, we continued to live in an atmosphere that was oppressive. As the German army continued its astounding success in the USSR, rumors were flying that hundreds of prominent French Jews had been arrested in their homes. It was December 1941.

A few weeks earlier, the exhibit "Jews and France" was shown in the Palais Berlitz. Compelled by curiosity, I went to see what it was about. An entire range of odious propaganda was on display. I could not imagine where it could all lead. I remember very clearly being divided between anger and amusement by the ridiculous caricatures and utter stupidity in general. How could people believe such inanity? Grotesque faces were displayed along with photos and descriptive captions filled with hatred. I was Jewish, as were my parents and many of my friends, as well as my father's boss and his wife. What did they have in common with the hideous monsters on these display panels? Nothing, absolutely nothing. And what was the "dominating power" they kept talking about and showing from every angle? I had trouble seeing what kind of danger I, a future die maker, son of a cap maker, could present. It was ludicrous.

Despite all the signs, I was relatively unconscious of what was going on. I refused to wear the yellow star. My mother continued to encourage me to concentrate on my schoolwork, and I did not focus on what was going on around me. I tried to handle my new role as "man of the house" as well as I could since my father's departure. In the beginning of 1942, after my father had been arrested by the French gendarmes and incarcerated in the camp at Mérignac-Beaudésert, my mother was left without any resources. As I learned in a letter dated February 18, 1942, found at YIVO, from the commissioner at the work site to an executive of the UGIF, the separation indemnity the workers received would no longer be given as of January 31, 1942. The men had been arrested by "occupation authorities." Occupation authorities! . . . So much bad faith was beyond belief.

My mother took some steps to receive aid from the UGIF. I found papers about this at the Centre de Documentation Juive Contemporaine (CDJC, Center for Contemporary Jewish Documentation). A woman came to the house to interview my mother and beginning April 29, 1942, we received a little money to help us get by: 400 francs a month. But it wasn't enough; our rent was then 300 francs a month. As I had just completed my third year at Dorian and was a full-fledged tool-and-die maker, my mother asked me to give up my project of doing another year of technical drafting. Landing a job would be preferable. Thanks to the reputation of Dorian technical school, I was employed by Caudron, an airplane manufacturer in Boulogne Billancourt in southwest Paris. On August 4, 1942, as a young factory worker, I took my position at the vise, a job I disliked intensely. At the end of the year, I became a technical employee, paid by the month and no longer by the hour. The salary was much more attractive, and so was the work. I worked on technical drafts for plane assembly. Sometimes, I would make an extra copy for a colleague and leave it in an envelope discreetly placed at a specifically designated spot. The drawing would disappear. I had no idea where the drawing would end up, but I had the feeling I was helping the cause against the Germans since the work in the factory was for them. The Allies knew what we were manufacturing, and one day we were bombed in broad daylight. I barely got out alive.

As I said, I was rather unconscious of the things that were going on during the Occupation, at least until the end of 1941. It was a carefree attitude of youth that allowed me to scoff at the danger. But I began to understand exactly what was going on. When I was hired at the Caudron factory, I was careful not to say that I was Jewish, aware that it was an incentive not to hire me. And I knew full well that denunciations were very commonplace. Since I was not wearing the star, they did not ask if I was Jewish. They just looked at my highly valued diplomas from Dorian and the positive results of the vise exam they had me take. I also realized the risk I was taking by not wearing the star. In my neighborhood, I always made sure to carry something in front of my chest where the star should have been, in case I met someone I knew.

In mid-July 1942, the major roundup began. This time women and children were arrested. They were taken to the Vélodrome d'Hiver, a bicycle stadium where I once went with my father to watch a race. Nothing was provided in this big stadium to accommodate the thousands of people who had been arrested. Once again, the French police distinguished themselves by conscientiously fulfilling their vile duty. They followed orders, all of them to the letter with a professionalism that was exemplary.

Apart from belonging to the UGIF, the only thing that seemed to protect a Jewish family was a German *ausweis* (safe-conduct pass), given to those whose husbands made sheepskin jackets for the Germany military on the eastern front. The Jews with an *ausweis* were left untouched by the French police. But in our case, and we were among the majority, no such "privilege" existed. We had to hide if we heard a roundup was coming, whether it was just a rumor or not. The threat was constant, and sometimes my mother and I would find ourselves in the huge apartment where my friend

Jacquot's grandparents lived. We naïvely believed that we had nothing to fear since they were so old.

During this period, the war in the east was raging at its worst. To mitigate the brutal attacks that the Soviets were subjected to, the USSR requested a second front. The Allies did not seem ready yet and offered only lip service. The German army, proud of its continued glorious victories celebrated by the French press, Radio Paris, and all the little *führers* from Bucard to Doriot (notorious French collaborators), reached the outer limits of Leningrad (St. Petersburg), then Moscow, then Stalingrad (Volgograd). This disaster went on for months and added to our pessimism.

A tiny glimmer of hope came at the beginning of 1943. The Red Army, which managed to encircle Field Marshal Friedrich von Paulus's German army at Stalingrad after months of intense fighting and extensive bloodshed, obtained a surrender on February 2, 1943. In spite of this, the siege of Leningrad continued with the same intensity.

Probably in order to protect me, my mother maintained her silence with regard to my father. Who knows how I would have reacted to the truth. The war in the east continued to rage with a sort of apathy settling in on both sides. The Allies still had not landed in the west. On the other hand, the local roundups of Jews occurred increasingly often, and the French police carried out their despicable work.

At this point, we were living in constant fear of being arrested. And what seemed inevitable did finally take place. One month after my father's arrest (my mother was unaware of it), on the night of February 3, 1944, an interminable night, we were awakened at two in the morning. Someone was banging on our door . . . for a long time . . . louder and louder, faster and faster. It did not take us long to realize what was happening. With a resigned expression on her face, almost relieved that what we had been expecting for so long had finally come, my mother opened the door to two uniformed policemen, who barged into our apartment. She probably hoped as she turned the doorknob that it was something else. But that hope was dashed in an instant. When she saw the French policemen who had come to arrest us, she raced over to the window. The officers grabbed her waist, stopping her from jumping. We had to get dressed and take only few belongings, which were stated on a list read to us. A plainclothes officer was waiting for us downstairs, and all three of them took us to the police precinct at place Baudoyer, next to the local city hall in the 4th arrondissement.

Other people who had already been arrested were filling the police station. Our papers and our belongings were checked. After a moment, a policeman came over to me. He said we had forgotten to bring some blankets. They decided I would return to the house with an escort and get them. Off we went. Rue de Rivoli, rue du Temple, rue Geoffroy l'Angevin. Four hundred yards. Four hundred deserted yards, because the night curfew was in effect. That short distance seemed to last an eternity. I walked beside the police officer. He must have been the same age as my father. I was thinking . . . *I could easily push him over and then run off, disappear into the night. I knew the neighborhood inside out. I could lose him in a few seconds. Just disappear . . . and leave my mother in the police precinct? My mother. What would become of her without me? My father had already disappeared; could I do the same thing? Wasn't it my duty to remain by her side? She was terrified, living in fear of this night for so many months. I wanted to escape to hit this bastard and run . . . run. I repeated this phrase constantly. And I thought of my mother constantly. Hadn't she just tried, not even an hour before, to put an end to her life?* We arrived at the apartment building. The officer got the keys from the concierge, and we walked up three flights of stairs. I got the blankets and closed the door. He returned the keys to the concierge. We were on the street again. And still the questions rolled around in my head. Run? Stay? Rue du Temple, rue de Rivoli. I bent down as if to tie my shoelace. I was mulling it over. He waited. I could pounce on him, push him over and run off. I got up slowly. I began walking again. I couldn't leave her. Place Baudoyer. The police precinct. I took my place by my mother's side.

Today, I am very happy that I did not run away. I don't think I could have lived without knowing what happened to her, without knowing that it was impossible for me to save her. If I had run away, I would have lived with the idea, a terrible burden, that if I had stayed maybe I could have saved her. Having made this choice, I know now that it was impossible to save her. I remained with her until the end, until the last moment. That night, that choice, determined the rest of my life.

Later, much later, when I would think back to that terrible night, I wondered if the policemen were actually providing me a chance to escape by having me return to the apartment with an escort that I could have easily dumped. But no. They could have even let me go home alone. They knew I would not run away since my mother remained a hostage in the police precinct.

I shall never forget that night or that police precinct. When I was a child, we often passed it when the three of us would walk to the Seine for a stroll. And it still exists. There is a plaque on it today that reads:

They

died

along

the

road to

Liberation

August 19 to 24, 1944

Bardon, Charles (Sergeant)

Chuet, Gaston (Sergeant)

Pezin, Charles (Sergeant)

Vançon, Emile (Sergeant)

Salvat, Auguste (Inspector)

Gagnepain, Edmond (Officer)

Paris, Paul (Officer)

DO NOT FORGET

Can six days of heroism by a few redeem four years of vile actions for the majority? Can a Legion of Honor for six days of heroism erase four years of dishonor shrouded in a veil of silence even today?

When I conducted my research at the Center for Contemporary Jewish Documentation on rue Geoffroy l'Asnier, three hundred yards from the police precinct, I found the arrest order from that cursed night. It was a document signed by France's version of Adolf Eichmann, the director of the infamous municipal police, named Hennequin. He was responsible for the detailed instructions written out for the Vélodrome d'Hiver roundup. The arrest order was dated February 3, 1944. In order to alleviate any problems with their conscience, the policemen who were given this miserable task were told they were arresting "Jews and Jewesses who were foreign or without a country whose information was attached." But a slight subtlety was added: among those who were to be arrested were "all Jewish members of the family, particularly children under the age of sixteen, even if there is no file card on them." In other words, French Jews as well. This was my case.

Let's look closely at the arrest order. After the list of potential dispensations—"half-Jewish children from Aryan spouse," etc.—and a telephone number of the Office of Jewish Affairs, in case of questionable instances, the arrest order read as follows:

> The operation will begin on February 3 at 11:00 pm and will be carried out until complete execution.
>
> You will receive a certain number of file cards to arrest [*sic*], some tape to affix the seal on the door which is henceforth condemned, one per home, transportation orders for Drancy, sheets of white paper upon which the arrest teams will note down their observations, if necessary, with regard to the special cases they might encounter.

With respect to setting up arrest teams, "Each arrondissement will organize arrest squads with the aid of its own personnel and reinforcements brought in from outside: "inspectors from the *police judiciaire* [the detective branch of the police], inspectors from the *renseignements généraux* [the branch of the police force dealing with political security], policemen in uniform as well as plainclothes." . . . No one was left out.

Roundup and transfer

The arrested Jews will be conducted to police precincts. Each police district superintendent will receive one or more buses at 6:30 am and it will be his job to manage the transfer of the Jews within his district; the Jews will then be taken to the internment camp Drancy, with the help of these vehicles. When the district has finished the transfers, it will then notify headquarters before returning the buses.

An adequate team will be assigned to each bus. The windows of the bus will remain closed and the platform will be reserved to the belongings.

Special orders

The head of squad, after having verified the identity of the individuals that he has arrested, will not enter into discussion with them under any circumstances.

He will bring them to the designated police precinct and will make certain they will bring the possessions mentioned below.

The possessions were the following:

Their identity card and . . . all other family papers considered useful, food ration cards, food and textile ration tickets. The following goods and possessions: two blankets, a pair of shoes, two shirts, two pairs of socks, two underpants, a work outfit, a pair of sheets, a cup, a can if possible, a set of forks and knives for meals, toiletries (a razor is allowed). Enough food provisions for at least two days; they can bring more if they want. Not more than one suitcase of medium size for food. The blankets will be slung over the shoulders, the goods and possessions from the above list will be placed in one bag or suitcase, in total two suitcases or packages, one being for food provisions.

The head of the squad will be in charge of the implementation.

Opening the doors

If upon your arrival there is no response when you knock, the door should be broken down to make sure nobody is there.

Sealing the apartment

If the Jews are absent from their home for whatever reason, it should be duly noted on the file card and the concierge or the neighbors should be informed of their responsibilities. However, it is evident that if the apartment is empty of furniture, it should not be sealed.

However, it is necessary to verify this beforehand.

That night, the number of arrests planned for Paris was the following:

1st arrondissement : 6
2nd arrondissement : 56

3rd arrondissement : 256

4th arrondissement : 228

5th arrondissement : 22

6th arrondissement : 6

7th arrondissement : 1

8th arrondissement : 3

9th arrondissement : 62

10th arrondissement : 239

11th arrondissement : 405

12th arrondissement : 45

13th arrondissement : 28

14th arrondissement : 18

15th arrondissement : 25

16th arrondissement : 7

17th arrondissement : 23

18th arrondissement : 189

19th arrondissement : 199

20th arrondissement : 424

In all, 2,242 Jews were to be arrested, by more than a thousand policemen—all French. The Vichy government had requested and obtained authorization for the police to remain exclusively in charge and take full responsibility for "maintaining order and national security." This was active collaboration . . . especially when you consider that it allowed the German army to "spare" a thousand men who could then be free to fight on the eastern front.

The organization was flawless. At 6:30 a.m., we were loaded onto a city bus and driven to Drancy to be handed over to the gendarmes. I never suspected that such a place existed. The U-shaped buildings are still there today. A camp was established in the middle of them.

There were at least a dozen different stairwells. Prisoners were on every level. The administrative office was located at the base of the U, toward the left. This is where we were directed upon our arrival. After they took possession of our money and jewelry (a receipt was issued), the men and women were separated, and we waited. What were we waiting for? We didn't know. We waited. We only knew that our incarceration at Drancy was only temporary and that we were to be sent elsewhere. We heard something about a work camp. We could mingle freely among each other, and we all talked of this destination, reassuring ourselves and trying to understand. But we had no further information. The people who had been in Drancy the longest claimed they had no idea. Our only certainty was that we had lost control over our destiny. We had no more say whatsoever. Did it matter anyway? When would we be leaving? Nobody could tell us. Where would we go? "To *Pitchipoï*,"[2] declared the oldest ones with amusement. So we awaited our departure for *Pitchipoï*. The day after our arrival at Drancy, February 5, 1944, was my eighteenth birthday. What a sad birthday. I went to see my mother in her stairwell. She was strong, but resigned and very concerned for my future.

The waiting soon ended. Some of the men were gathered and had their hair cut. I had trouble with this sudden urge for grooming. I was very fond of my hair, and this haircut made me realize that I was no longer free. It was also a definitive sign that our departure was imminent. On February 10, 1944, barely a week after our arrival, we were packed like sardines into cattle cars. The hour of departure for *Pitchipoï* had come. In the middle of this cattle car

---

2. *Pitchipoï* is an imaginary, idyllic village in Yiddish folk tales. It was commonly referred to in the French transit camp at Drancy as the Jews anticipated being sent on to an unknown and dreaded destination.

was a large container that would serve as a latrine bucket. We barely had enough space to sit down. My mother was near me. A minuscule opening designed for horses (these railroad cars were originally intended for them) let in a narrow shaft of light and a little air. It also allowed us to estimate the passing time, to distinguish if it was day or night, and to count the days. It was the middle of winter, but the heat was stifling. We were thirsty and tried not to think about it; the two buckets of water provided were quickly empty. The train stopped very often, and each time, the steam engine whistle would blow with short repeated blasts. Had we arrived at *Pitchipoï*? Were we going to get out? Would the train continue? I cannot hear that piercing sound today without it sending chills up my spine. At times, I still hear the whistles ringing in my ears . . . and I see my mother.

During one of these stops, there was a lot of noise. The doors were opened. We were in the middle of the German countryside. The German soldiers had some of us get down from the car for a few minutes. We were dazed, but we quickly got over it in order to take advantage of the time to clean up the cesspit in which we were traveling. Each hour the odor had become more and more unbearable. Then we departed again. And the stops began again, but we were kept in the cars. And with the sound of the whistle each time, the same question would arise: Had we arrived in *Pitchipoï*?

During one of these stops, longer than the others, I was able to hoist myself up to the opening and look outside. Dawn was about to break. It was the third day of our "journey." Hanging from the window by the strength of my arms, I looked out. I could read the name of the station where we had stopped: Auschwitz. We had not arrived in *Pitchipoï*.

THE DESCENT INTO HELL

Auschwitz-Birkenau

In fact, the train continued . . . but not for long this time. A few minutes later, it came to a stop once again, and we began to hear a lot of commotion and the sound of the train doors opening. Orders were shouted. The sound grew closer and suddenly, with a frightful racket, our door slid open with a heavy thud. The light was blinding. A desolate countryside covered in snow spread out before us. There was no vegetation. Was this just another stop? Had we finally arrived in *Pitchipoï*? To get onto the platform, we had to jump. Then we had to help the less agile people get down. I wanted to take our suitcases, but I was told to leave them. We had to leave everything behind. Hands from outside were offered to help us down. I jumped to the ground and looked around. These helping hands were attached to bodies, people dressed in striped outfits. We had arrived. I was standing by my mother, whom I had helped off the train. We began to hear a few whispered words in Yiddish that these costumed people were murmuring to everybody. *"Zay gesund"*—*Be in good health*. What did this mean? Why were they greeting us with the traditional words for good-bye? This could not be what they meant. But why should we be in good health? And why were they saying it so discreetly, in a whisper, so that the few Germans in uniform surveying the situation could not hear? Where were we? My mother and I were quickly separated since each sex was directed to a separate line. We would see each other later. Everyone in line was standing at ease. I had no idea what time it could be. We began to advance. The snow crunched under my feet, and it reminded me of how my mother had spoken of the countryside of her youth. I looked across at her now as I walked, and she, in her line of women, looked across at me. We looked at each other, without really looking, our expressions vacant. We marched forward because we had to march, everyone in their line because the men and the women were no longer together. No one explained anything to us. We knew nothing, we understood nothing. We did what the others did, what the gestures commanded us to do, what the shouts seemed to order us to do. "*Los! Los!*" Hurry up! Let's go! And I was still looking at my mother, and she was still looking at me. "*Schnell! Schnell!*" Hurry up! Faster! We speeded up when the order was shouted and the others marched more quickly. I was still looking toward my mother, whom I could barely see by now. With the other women, she was being directed toward trucks. They climbed in. I was relieved to see that at least she would not have to go by foot. She was very tired.

I continued to walk. We arrived in front of a huge gate with barbed wire running across it that look electrified. This was the camp entrance. Had we now arrived in *Pitchipoï*? Behind the gate, there were brick buildings and above the entrance written in wrought iron was the phrase: *Arbeit macht frei.* I did not understand anything, but soon all that I had experienced would come together—the people wearing striped outfits when we got off the train, the *zay gesund,* marching into the camp, the trucks, etc. But I began to understand one thing when I read *Arbeit macht frei.* This "Work makes you free" made me understand something that I can only explain in one way. I said to myself at that moment, "They are mocking us." What irony! What sadism! But I moved along with the others as the orders were shouted out, managing as best I could with all the pushing and the constant blows that rained down, and would continually do so. We entered, and as we walked, almost running, between the shouts, hits and pushing and shoving that urged us forward, I smelled something in the air . . . an odor of plucked chicken over a flame. I was hungry. We had been traveling for three days and three nights. It was February 13, 1944, a Sunday. We were now waiting in front of a building. I saw those at the head of the line undressing. Then everyone began to undress. I did as everyone else. A mountain of clothes soon formed next to the line. Inside the building, the first men in line were being shaved. Head, body, pubic hair. I waited my turn, naked in the snow, hiding my nakedness as best I could . . . hiding what was still mine and most intimate to me. But I would soon have to relinquish that as well, leaving me nothing. I was not yet conscious of what was taking place. It was appallingly cold. Then I entered the building. I was shaved. With the others, I waited, once again in front of another building where the men at the head of the line were walking out, soaking wet. We were going to wash. It was my turn to go in. After the hot shower, I went out into the freezing snow once again, trying to dry off as best I could. And then I waited in line again, in this bitter cold weather. There was yet another building where I waited for my striped outfit and my wooden clogs. Nothing was in my size. I tried to exchange one outfit for a better fit amidst shouts and hits. It seemed we could not do anything fast enough. I wrapped my foot in rags as I saw the others doing, and I slipped on the clogs that would soon become agonizing on my feet. Then we went out. Dressed like this, I had now entered into this new world. I looked like a clone of everyone else. I was a little less cold than before. There was another building. I waited in line. Everyone in this line was receiving a tattoo. I did not wonder about it. I just rolled up my sleeve as the others had done and I waited. Like the others in front of me, I would have a number on my arm. My identity was the only thing left to me. And they stripped me of that as well.

I was still breathing in the odor I had noticed when I entered. I was hungry. It was Sunday. I saw one of the men in a striped outfit talking with someone else in the line. He was speaking French. As the line advanced and I came up to him, he asked me about the latest news in France. I told him there was talk of an Allied landing. Before he could get another question out, I wanted to sound him out. Was this sweet smell a meal they were preparing for us? A few seconds went by. No answer. I asked him another question: "My mother . . . when will I be able to see her again?" He looked at me without much expression on his face. "When was she born?"

"In 1895."

"So she is . . . forty-nine years old. You should forget about your mother."

It felt as if I had been hit over the head with a ton of bricks. I understood now. Everything, not in detail, but I understood. For a few seconds I did not understand . . . or rather, I understood, but I could not comprehend. I did not want to comprehend it. But this confusion lasted only a few seconds. The serious tone with which the striped outfit spoke wiped away any doubt. I had understood. And I needed to know more. The line advanced. I turned around. The striped outfit was too far away. There was another one farther along. I waited until the line reached him. It was taking an eternity. The line seemed to have come to a standstill. I needed to know. When I was finally near him, I did not give him the chance to talk to me. "Did they kill my mother? She was born in 1895." He did not answer. "How?" He muttered, "Gas." My world fell apart. In an instant. I had not understood or seen a thing before. When we walked in these two lines, the uniformed Germans were watching us and making a selection. Those too young, not young enough, the sick and the weak, were spotted and set aside. They were loaded into trucks and delivered to their death. *Zay gesund.* I understood. I was stunned, shaken, no longer thinking. I could not scream, or cry, or fight. Why? How? These questions did not even graze my consciousness. It all spun around in my head in a few seconds. The striped outfit may have said something to me, but I did not hear him. . . . My mother . . . . Then all of a sudden I thought of my father again. Maybe he was here. I asked him, "Maurice Michlin?" He shook his head. Then he asked:

"What was his job?"

"Cap maker."

He smiled.

"Me too."

Then taking a more serious tone:

"We don't need any cap makers here. You need a useful job here. *"Schreibst du deutsch?"* (Do you write German?)"

"A little."

He seemed a bit uneasy.

"Do you have a profession?"

"Tool-and-die maker."

He told me that Siemens, the huge German conglomerate that included engineering and electrical companies, was looking for workers. He slapped me on the shoulder and walked off. I was in line waiting for my tattoo. My mind was blank, but I had understood two things. I understood what *Pitchipoï* was. And I understood that I had become a nonentity.

And I also understood that I would have to live with this and accept what was and find a way out. There was no choice!

My new name was now inscribed on the upper side of my left forearm: 173 847.

I was part of another world. I had to learn to understand it and find my place. But most important of all, I had to forget everything of my life before I arrived, at least temporarily. I had to accept what the striped outfit, an inmate like myself, had told me: not to think about my mother anymore. I knew I would need to listen and be alert in order to figure out the rules that I had to play by to avoid being beaten and stay clear of this constant threat of death, which was so close and so present.

The first night, after a meal consisting of a slice of brown bread and kielbasa, a type of Polish sausage, which would be the only thing on the menu for months on end, I slept. It was the only respite from the constant battering between the time we got up until we got into bed at night. We were in brick buildings that had originally been Polish barracks. We slept in wooden bunk beds—simple boards placed horizontally on three superimposed levels. Each level was two yards wide and we slept six to a level. We were packed in like sardines, with one cover for all. Sleeping like this, pressed against each other and the wood slats, it was not a good idea to move. If one of us decided to turn, it forced the other five to turn also.

The first night was over. At the registration I was asked what my profession was, and I responded "*Feinmechaniker*," as the inmate told me to the day before. Then I went to the area where Siemens was recruiting. After a long wait, a German officer gave me an exam. I had to describe the top, front, and side views of a mechanical piece drawn on technical paper he showed me. Then I had to read the diameter of an object handed to me with a micrometer caliper. Dorian school and Caudron manufacturing plant in a nutshell. Child's play, even in my elementary German. I was hired immediately. I was now going to work for Siemens. But before starting that job, I was told, the factory had to be built first.

My striped outfit now bore the number that had been tattooed on my arm the day before along with the Jewish symbol, the Star of David, made from a red triangle pointing downward upon which was sewn a yellow triangle pointing upward. I was now a full-fledged *häftling* (inmate).

Soon, along with a few other inmates hired by Siemens, I was transferred to another camp—Birkenau. This is where we had first arrived. The transfer took place on foot, and we retraced the steps we had taken after our arrival. Birkenau was an immense camp with wooden barracks, each about forty yards by ten yards. We were assigned to block 11, which was a *Strafkommando* block. The *Strafkommando* was a disciplinary unit, in other words, in the world of Auschwitz, a group to be broken in. The rules baffled me. Had I made the right choice? I was chosen to work for Siemens and thought that doing familiar work would soften the harsh regime. Yet, I was being punished. What was the punishment? And why? What kind of world was this? The first few days were very anxious ones. But as time went by, we began to think that we had simply been dumped here at random. Later, we understood that our presence in *kommando* block 11 had allowed Siemens to keep us on call. And most importantly, they were assured that we would remain alive.

A Jew who was punished was not sent to a *Strafkommando*. He was immediately hanged or "selected." Selection meant systematic elimination of the weakest Jews by gas. They were called *musulmans* in the camp jargon. Emaciated and haggard, the cachexia, the physical wasting and malnutrition these men suffered from had left them listless. We were safe from selection because it did not exist in block 11.

With time, I realized I had made the right choice. I was able to survive thanks to my poor father, to whom I shall remain eternally grateful for making me into a tool-and-die maker. As a doctor or an actor, I would have been gassed upon my arrival or else been rapidly eliminated by the terrible work regime that crushed the Jewish inmates who did not have a "useful" skill. A few doctors and musicians found positions in the camp. Doctors became nurses at the hospital, and musicians made up the camp orchestra. But their numbers were restricted and once the required number was attained, the others were done away with.

Most importantly, this job allowed me to belong to a group. To find oneself in the midst of a hostile and unknown world— which was the fate of most—was to face horrible odds for survival. If you did not speak German or Polish or belong to some sort of group that provided psychological support, it was impossible to keep going. People were subjected to working ten to twelve hours a day of hard manual labor on an empty stomach, to dealing with the bitter cold, and were at the mercy of vicious *kapos* (capos, chiefs), who thought only of their own survival and freely gave beatings when the mood took them. The harshness of this way of life promised death at the end of the road. And that road was a short one. It took no more than three or four months.

In the Siemens *kommando,* we had the advantage of being part of a group that shared the same destiny. Moreover, our group included about twenty French-speaking inmates, which meant that we could give each other moral support. Of course, the hellish environment in the camp was the same for us all, except for certain *prominents* (privileged ones—inmates who were part of the hierarchy set up by the SS to run the camp). Our common lot was the lack of adequate food along with an intense fatigue causing us to lose twenty pounds or more in a few weeks. The blows dealt out on our work site were less frequent than most, but were quite severe once we returned to our block if we did not bend to the will of the block leader fast enough.

Belonging to this Siemens *kommando* was a chance for us to keep our connection with the life we had left behind. Working allowed us to hold onto our dignity and remain human beings. We of the Siemens *kommando* were the only Jews in block 11. The other *kommandos* in the block were made up of non-Jews, who were there for disciplinary reasons. It was easy to tell what "category" the others belonged to. Each of them, like us, wore a sign on his breast that represented the "group" to which he was assigned. We had the red and yellow star. Political prisoners wore a red triangle pointing downward; common criminal prisoners, a green triangle; homosexuals, a pink triangle; saboteurs, a black triangle. Most of the inmates in block 11 had red or green triangles. They were the quasi "aristocracy" in the camp; we Jews were the pariahs. Only the Jews were cut off from the world outside. Political and criminal inmates would sometimes receive letters and packages with food to compensate for the meager rations we were all given. Naturally we were banned from even gathering the crumbs of the "feasts" the Poles would enjoy. They were the majority in the block. We watched them eat, and they would savor their food with ostentatious pleasure. I dreamed about the onions they received on a regular basis. For me, onions became the symbol of strength, good health, and even life, and remain so today.

These first few days allowed me to get a sense of where I was: in Poland, Upper Silesia, a territory annexed by the Third Reich, which explains why some SS were Polish. As I looked around the camp, I was struck by the fact that there was not a shred of paper anywhere, no pencils, no mirrors, no way of telling time. This camp was a nightmare. All men wore striped outfits. Gaunt, with shaved heads, they dragged themselves around in exhaustion. Many looked as if they were close to death. There seemed to be no way out. Those who were not gassed were killed from overwork after a few weeks. One would have to be strong, endure hunger, cold, suffering, humiliation, and beatings. We tried to cling to life and maintain our humanity in this perfect system designed to strip us of everything by reducing us to the level of beasts ready to kill each other, willing to accept anything in order to prolong our existence. I would have to fight for myself, struggle to control my emotions, and not let them take my life, my carcass. And most importantly, I would need to remain a man, forget nothing, and maintain my dignity. I would have to hold on . . . not become an animal or even worse, a nonhuman.

I began to understand how the camp functioned, gradually learning the system and the rules that had to be followed in order to stay alive. I discovered an important word that would soon become familiar: *organisieren.* To "organize" meant to barter, to swap whatever you could for something that could be vital for personal survival. Many people bartered part of their day's food ration for a cigarette. But one could also barter a service for food, like taking on a task and making oneself useful to a Polish inmate who had just received a package. I had nothing to barter so I had to stick to my meager rations.

The hierarchy was very strong, oppressive, and cleverly thought out to exacerbate primitive emotions. The SS, the top of the pyramid, would rarely make an appearance except in watchtowers or to accompany the *kommandos* outside the camp. All the power was delegated to the inmates, mainly the German common criminal inmates. From the head of the camp, the *lagerältester,* down to the head of the block, the *blockältester,* aided by a *schreiber* (secretary), the camp was strictly organized. Each section had its own chief, the *stubedienst,* with each level being responsible to the next higher rank. And each one, depending on his importance, took advantage of whatever small privileges he could grab. For example, bread was not directly distributed to each inmate, but was instead given to the head of the block, who then divided it up among the section heads. The latter then gave the remaining portions to the men under them. The head of the block helped himself to a generous portion, and the section heads then had their turn. The rest was then divided up among the inmates. It was too bad for the inmates whose *blockältester* had a hearty appetite or who did not like them. Injustice was thus encouraged as part of the system, and slavishness became a way of life in order to get a better portion of food. These "masters" had their own rooms, along with personal tailors who made them clothes fitted to their measurements. They also had helpers, chosen from the youngest inmates, the *pipel,* who were veritable house servants . . . and sometimes more.

These masters had practically absolute power over the ordinary inmates—power over life and power over death. They could starve one of us if they wanted, or offer favoritism to another in order to buy his services. Bread for us was something essential. In fact, bread sent me into an existential quandary. Should I eat it all at once or carefully break it into pieces and eat it throughout the day to create the illusion that I was eating more often? This preoccupation was quickly resolved. By keeping it, I ran the risk of having it stolen. Food was the main topic of our conversations. We were continually hungry. The rations hardly sufficed, and they were the same for everyone, big or small. Everyone lost a little weight each day. I noticed that as time went on the taller men would waste away faster. Rations were even more inadequate for them.

Our *blockältester,* Bednarek, a Polish red triangle, was a real sadist. Things were never to his liking. Nothing was ever clean enough. The blankets had to be put away properly, but were systematically tossed on the ground as he judged them poorly folded or improperly placed. This was excuse enough for beating the men belonging to that bunk. Even today I still remember a Polish order we often heard: "*dvadjeshapinche inadupé,*" twenty-five lashes on the ass. With this order came a "ceremony" that was an unbearable ritual. In the courtyard between our block and block 13, adjacent to ours, stood a table specially designed for this outrageous punishment. A strap was slipped over the feet and hands, attaching the person to the table. Lying at a right angle on the table, with arms and legs outstretched, the inmate could no longer move. He was ready to receive the whipping. When this "ceremony" took place, we had to stand in rows and watch the painful spectacle. Soon the thin body would be covered with bruises that would begin to bleed, and the inmate would scream out in pain with each incredibly brutal whack. The ritual seemed to last an eternity. Afterward, the poor fellow had to get up, which he rarely could do. This was a clear message to us, and we accepted anything in order to avoid being the one tied down to the table.

How many times did we hear the order shouted to get up and hurry into the courtyard? We knew we were about to be treated to a "session," but we seldom knew why. One time, there was no reason at all. Bednarek and his underlings must have been bored one night and wanted to have some fun by getting us to run around for a few hours. We were asleep after a harsh day of work. In the middle of the night, Bednarek, who was probably drunk, started to shout. It did not take us long to wake up, get down from the bunks and hurry to the door. The punishing blows were distributed freely. We were all running, pushing our way out the narrow door that could take only one person at a time. We scrambled over the men who fell to avoid being beaten from behind and also to avoid the two *kapos* standing to the right and left of the door. It was a real panic. Once we were outside, the shouts came again commanding us to return inside. And the same routine would start up again. Beatings from behind, beatings as we passed through the door, and beatings upon arrival into the barrack. And the game started anew . . . one, two, three times. More inmates were killed that terrible night, gratuitously, simply because our *blockältester* and his henchmen had nothing better to do. Unwarranted sadistic actions such as this were commonplace and we were the victims.

I remember another scene. One day an SS officer was walking by and pointed to an inmate who happened to be nearby. He indicated for him to approach. When he did, the SS took his gun from the holster and gave him a violent pistol-whipping to the skull. After a few blows, the inmate collapsed. The SS commanded him to get up and each time, the moment he got to his feet, the beating would resume until he fell again. After a while, judging it enough, the officer put away his weapon and walked off, leaving the man in a pool of blood on the ground. His only crime had been to cross the path of the SS officer. Another story comes to mind. A *prominent,* in a tailor-made black uniform, had a favorite pastime. He would go to the latrine barracks (wooden planks with holes that ran the length of the building) and whip the men inside. He always shouted: *"Arsch mit ohren!"* Ass with ears!

Along with this ever-present brutality, the threat of the gas chamber hung over our heads. The four Auschwitz gas chambers were there in Birkenau. We knew that only Jews could be gassed, and it was made certain we did not forget it. If we were sent there, we knew we would depart by the squat, square smokestacks of the crematoriums that continually spit out a thick smoke licked by flames. The pervasive sweetish odor of burning flesh shrouded the camp and its surroundings. We also quickly learned that it was "unhealthy" to get sick. Going to the *Krankenbau,* the hospital, meant for any Jew the move toward eternity.

Death was everywhere—in the air, in the incessant black smoke from the crematorium smokestacks, near the blocks and in the blocks. Dead corpses were left in front of the barracks, and the *kommando* in charge of removing them did not always have the time to fulfill its task rapidly enough. Death, and the death of those around us, no longer meant very much. We quickly got used to the lifeless bodies strewn here and there, tangled and twisted. It was part of the scenery. Seeing this for the first time was virtually

unbearable. But soon, after seeing it often enough, it lost all meaning . . . an efficient dehumanization process masterminded by the
SS of the "Great German Reich."

We tried to find out about the other *kommandos*. We learned, for
example, who the people were who helped us off the trains when
we arrived. They were part of the Canada *kommando*. Their job was
to clean the train so that it could depart without delay. Cleaning
meant not only washing the train down, but also clearing out the
newcomers' belongings. They were then responsible for going
through these things, which often contained food. Naturally, they
would take some for themselves. This was another of the sources for
the barter system, along with packages that the non-Jews received.

We also learned there was a staff in charge of the gas chambers
and crematoriums: the *Sonderkommando,* the special command.
Their job was to clear out the gas chambers after the people had
been gassed and bring the dead bodies to the crematoriums. The
Sonderkommando, I soon discovered, lodged in block 13 next to our
own. The fact that they were so close disturbed me. What a loathsome job they had! In talking with fellow inmates, we would pass
on whatever information we were able to gather. We learned that
the gas, in crystal form, was tossed through air ducts into the large
room where the new arrivals, all naked, expected to take a "shower."
Once the crystals hit the air they emitted an asphyxiating gas.
Struggling for air, people would climb on top of each other and
become a tangled mass that the men from the *Sonderkommando*
would have to pull apart. One evening, Leon Ichbiah, one of my
friends, was distraught when he returned to the block. He told us
that a member of the *Sonderkommando* reported that among the
cadavers removed from the gas chamber, he had recognized Leon's

wife and daughter. What an abomination. Leon was devastated. He had suspected this fate was reserved for his wife and daughter. He knew it was true, as I knew that the inmate was telling me the truth upon my arrival when he said that my mother had been gassed because she was too "old." A man with an average constitution in a normal environment might cling to the hope, as slim as it may be, that those he cherished most in the world might survive, might by some miracle escape the selection and live, perhaps in another barrack or in another camp. But here, in this hell, this was totally unrealistic. And if this final hope did exist, it would certainly be snuffed out like a candle. Thus, I did not doubt that my mother had been gassed. I saw her climb into a truck. I had realized what that meant for some time now. And I had the same realization for my father, if he had come here. There were no Jewish inmates in the camp wearing glasses. Hope was not permitted . . . no longer permitted. The gas chamber was his final destination. It was necessary to face up to the facts no matter how harsh they were.

The friend from the *Sonderkommando* who told Leon this terrible news had known his wife and daughter very well. He could not have been mistaken. Leon believed in God and this helped him get through. But he nearly gave in to despair. We rallied around him and kept him going.

What a sad and nightmarish life the men in the *Sonderkommando* led in order to survive. Divided between disgust and pity, my heart bled for them. How could a man fall so low and demean himself by accepting the most horrible of all tasks? But did he have a choice? Could he have acted differently? Shouldn't he save himself? Could he refuse the work? Revolt? And then in his turn be one of the bodies to be removed from the gas chamber. But is it possible to live at this price? The desire to know obsessed me. With a friend, I discreetly went into block 13 as Leon had done, even though we were formally prohibited to do so. I wanted to understand this horror and deal with the reality of it. We met a French doctor there and had some discussions with him, but we never broached the essential topic. He gave us some bread. The *Sonderkommando* actually had abundant provisions obtained by the Canada *kommando* and by the new arrivals who managed to hold on to some food in spite of the formal orders upon arrival. They lived isolated from the rest of the camp. But in comparison to us, the accommodations were almost deluxe. The bunks were individual beds with mattresses. I got friendly with this doctor, but I never asked him any questions. I came to the realization that there was no point in knowing. And what was the point of judging? In this world, all previous frames of reference no longer existed. The rules were different. If we wanted to live, we needed to forget these old rules. Refusing the reality of the camp would be inevitably and rapidly welcoming death. This doctor was simply a man, like all of us, a man who wanted to live. That was enough for me. When I came down with scabies, it was he, in fact, who treated me. He gave me a jam jar filled with a curious golden liquid that I rubbed on my skin. In a few days I was cured.

The men working in the *Sonderkommando* had the misfortune of being assigned to carry out this heinous task. They were already part of another world and had to deal with this daily horror as best they could. They had nothing to do with the sadists running the camp. For the sadists, our suffering was their pleasure. Our bodies, bruised and beaten, were the proof of this.

During one of our trips inside Birkenau's vast complex, I discovered the women's camp, the Jewish Czech camp, and the Gypsy camp. The Czechs and the Gypsies lived with their families and wore regular civilian clothes. Their hair was not shaven. What a surreal scene within the surreal. Then, one day they were no longer there. The liquidation of the Czechs, who had been there for several months, took place in March 1944 to provide room for a new contingent from the Theresienstadt camp. The Gypsies were gassed after the annihilation of the Hungarian Jews. This is what the SS euphemistically called *sonderbehandlung*, special treatment.

All this information was not difficult to obtain even though the thousands who made up our ranks had very little contact with each other. One might wonder what part the SS played in filtering down this information in order to make us live in fear of death and render us docile slaves, submissive to their needs. However, when you think about it, this was not necessary. The smoke from the crematoriums was constantly present, along with the sirens signaling an escape and the display the next day at roll call when the fugitive, immediately caught, was hanged for all to see. This was enough to break our spirits and remind us of death, ever-present death that tangibly hung over our heads.

I never approached these gas chambers. I came very close once, in May 1944, when we finished the construction of the factory and our group moved, bringing with us our only belongings, that is, our spoons. We stopped at a mound, about five hundred yards from one of the four Birkenau *gaskammern* (gas chambers). I often think back to that day. We stopped to let an endless line of people go by. They were Hungarian Jews who had just arrived, walking slowly in rows of five, waiting their turn quietly in front of the building where another group had just entered. We watched them, unable to say a thing. We knew where they were going, but they had no idea. We knew they would enter that building and no one would come out. It was terrible. We knew and we did not say anything. We did not even think twice about it. We had nothing to say. It would not change a thing. Our group received the signal to move on. We began to walk, silently.

A few months earlier, in February 1944, soon after our arrival in Auschwitz, we had begun to build the Siemens factory. It was a few miles from Birkenau. The preexisting building there was in a state of ruin, with only the walls remaining. We had to reconstruct it and put a roof on top. Masons, carpenters and an architect were recruited from among the inmates in the camp outside of our *kommando*. Our work consisted of helping them. We carried sand, water, bricks, wood, and tiles in the cold and driving snow. Later, in April, we had to climb onto the roof and put the tiles in place. There was no respite. Our main concern was to find a free moment to steal away, so we could sit down in a corner, away from scrutiny, catch our breath and rest a little.

In the morning, every morning, seven days a week, we were awakened like all the other inmates at 4:30 a.m. The chime we heard in the distance was obtained by running a metal strip up and down inside a metal cylinder. "*Stavatch! Stavatch!*" We were ordered to get up in Polish. Now that we were up, all four hundred of us had to hurry to the "lavatories" together, one by one passing through the door where we were often beaten as we went into the courtyard. Then we had to wash as best we could, pouring water on ourselves with our hands. Then came the "coffee," a colored mixture without flavor or smell that we sometimes had to fetch when it came time to be on duty. On duty meant two of us would go to the kitchen and carry a barrel of about fifty quarts of boiling ersatz coffee over several hundred yards across slippery ground. At 5:30 a.m., we had to be ready. So we had an hour to get up, wash, and drink some of this filthy "coffee," clean our block, and make our bunk according to the prescribed rules. It meant racing through all of this. At six o'clock, after forming rows of five in the courtyard, we would leave the camp for work at the pace set by the orchestra made up of professional musicians who had miraculously escaped the gas chamber. They played SS marching songs and melancholy tunes that were popular then.

> J'attendrai, le jour et la nuit
> J'attendrai toujours, ton retour
> J'attendrai, J'attendrai
> Qu'un oiseau qui s'enfuit
> Vienne chercher l'oubli dans mon lit
> Le temps passe et court[1]

To this day I cannot bear this song. It made me clench my teeth because to me it was a real provocation. And still in rows of five, we would march in step accompanied by the SS and their dogs, toward the truck that would take us to the factory. Well before nightfall, we returned to the camp, greeted by the music of the orchestra. Well before nightfall because we had to go through the ordeal of roll call. Standing in the square, in rows of five, we had to stand at attention, *"Mützen ab!"* (caps off!), our caps held stiffly by our sides, while the SS counted us. This could last two hours and would continue until everybody was accounted for. We had to hold up the weak and the exhausted, who would sometimes collapse, not because they might be punished, but so they would not be forgotten and we would not have to start the roll call again in order to get the exact count. Sometimes, one of our friends would die during the roll call. We would have to hold him up so as not to slow down the counting process, and then bring him back into the barracks. We would divide up the bread he obviously no longer needed. It

---

1. I will wait day and night, I will wait for your return forever, I will wait, I will wait. . . .

allowed us to hold out a little longer. We learned to dominate our emotions.

In the evening once or twice a week, after an exhausting day, after the endless roll call, we would have to delay the thing we so desperately needed—going to sleep. First we had to delouse ourselves. Each of us had to scrupulously examine his few clothes and his blanket to make certain no lice had latched on. Lice carried typhus and were absolutely banned from the camp. The SS were scared to death of them, scared of being contaminated if an epidemic ever broke out. After this inspection, Bednarek, our sadistic *blockältester*, examined each and every one of us. Woe to the person with lice. The beatings would rain down and often a dead man's body, reduced to a pile of wounded flesh, was untied from the table.

Bobrek

In May 1944, we were moved since we had finished building the factory in which we were to work. Things were a little easier for us; we were less threatened by the prospect of death constantly bearing down. We had not done all this work for nothing. Siemens needed us. And we knew that in this new small camp, Bobrek, there was no gas chamber, no acrid odor hanging in the air as in Birkenau. The strict regime was the same, but there were no more beatings. And on Sundays, we could rest. Along with the usual slice of black bread and sausage, we were even given some "extra." Once a week we were served a soup with crushed peas in it. It reminded us that other flavors did exist. And this soup had the advantage, not negligible, of hardening and lasting for three days. We could save part of it and eat it over several days without fear of stealing. We were a small group and trusted each other.

No more than three hundred inmates occupied this small camp surrounded with barbed wire that was not electrified. We were placed in a large barrack attached to the factory. Another building was the kitchen, and a third one housed a small group of women who were in charge of maintaining the factory and the small garden, a little tract of land that could be tilled. The bunks were the same as in Birkenau and Auschwitz—just as uncomfortable. The factory was divided lengthwise into two nearly equal sections. On one side were the workbenches and the vises where I was stationed. On the other side were the machines: milling machines, grinding machines, lathes, etc. Even though the SS guarded us, the hierarchy was not as oppressive, and there was no longer the reign of terror as in

Birkenau. We worked all day under the direction of a foreman and
Bunsius, an engineer from Siemens, who had given me the basic
practical test the day after my arrival in the camp. What were we
making? We had no idea. Airplane parts? Submarine parts? I never
knew. My inmate friends, Prishkulnik and Bergeaud, had been engi-
neers before arriving in the camp and were responsible for quality
control. One day they were in some very serious trouble. As we
worked, two men arrived, dressed in long, black leather coats with
hats. This outfit was the telltale sign of the Gestapo. Prishkulnik was
called into the Siemens engineer's office. One of the parts that he
had approved turned out to be sabotaged. The agents from Berlin
wanted to execute him, but Bunsius vouched for him. We were very
frightened that day.

On Sundays we had free time, probably because our foreman and
Bunsius enjoyed having a day off. We seized the opportunity to
catch up on our sleep and later launch into long discussions on all
sorts of topics. We talked about the things that we missed the most:
Paris, often, but most often it was food.

We took advantage of these Sundays to get to know the various members of our Siemens *kommando:* Belgian, Polish, and
Dutch Jews. Albert Lacan (Lévy) often said that if one day we ever
got out of this hell, nobody would ever believe our story. How right
he was!

In Bobrek I got to know Itzhak, a Polish Jew who seemed to
have some difficulty walking. One day he told me what had happened to him in Auschwitz. They had asked for volunteers to do
light work with a generous food ration. He trustingly volunteered
and found himself in the medical experimentation block. They
subjected him to castration by burning off his testicles with a new

procedure invented by one of the SS doctors. After several months, he was barely getting over it and was happy to be still alive.

Bobrek was the lull in our passage through hell. As time went on, we began to feel the Germans getting edgy. We witnessed this with a great elation that almost made us forget the terrible Polish winter beginning to set in. The Soviets were advancing, we learned, and the German army was in disarray. This bit of news brought a breath of great optimism. We already saw ourselves back in Paris, living again. But what kind of life? Would I see my friends Jacquot, Henri, Félix, and Maxime? What had become of them? Had they escaped from the roundups? Were they in Auschwitz as well?

Our delight and expectation were great, but so was our anxiety. In fact, the threat of death that seemed to have disappeared for several months, reappeared in full force, and even more oppressive this time. When we talked among ourselves, imagining the defeat of our tormentors, we became concerned that they would liquidate us. It was obvious to us they could not leave behind any trace of their barbarism, and if they had to flee, they would not burden themselves with prisoners to slow down their escape. With this fear in our minds, one of us proposed the crazy idea of putting on a show for the end of the year. Naively, perhaps, we believed we could save our necks. The project was proposed to the SS, who accepted it. The French part of the show consisted of songs and the presentation of short plays. I volunteered to play a scene. For several weeks, we spent our Sundays preparing. We built a stage and practiced repeatedly so that we would be prepared. Because I could not write, since there was no paper and pencil in the camp, I reconstructed from memory Harpagon's monologue from *The Miser*, by Molière. When the day of the performance finally arrived, the SS were seated in the first row. They did not understand a word of French. My friend, Guy Lohac, sang several songs, one of which was "Douce France," and I did my monologue. The show was a triumph. The Soviets were moving closer every day.

Gleiwitz

A couple of weeks after the show, we were awakened at about one o'clock on the morning of January 18, 1945. Shouts rang out. Orders came to prepare our "things" and hurry out to the courtyard. We were going to join the inmates from Buna-Monowitz, the camp of I. G. Farben's industrial complex. The cold was unbearable. It must have been about -10°F, and it turned my nose into an icicle. I was sure my ears were going to fall off. We were each given an entire loaf of bread and a larger than usual portion of kielbasa. We did not need to wonder what was going on. The Red Army was obviously not very far away, and we were about to evacuate the camp. We waited . . . for hours . . . in the bitter Polish cold, on the slippery ground, wrapped in our blankets and clasping our bread tightly. Then we began to march. There were hundreds of us, in a line that seemed as if it would never end, flanked by armed SS. And we marched as best we could, encumbered by our bread. The order was clear. We had to march. There was no way we could forget it. Often, shots were heard along the way that would leave one of us dead, too exhausted to carry on. We marched like this for two days, fearing with every step that we would slip on the icy road. We walked over forty miles in two days, stopping only once along the way. The first night, a barn on a Polish farm in Nikolaïef served as a dormitory. We piled in and slept on the hay. Two friends, a Polish Jew and a French-speaking Austrian Jew, Zeev Steinfeld and Paul Schaffer, took advantage of the pitch-black night to hide in the hay and then run away. Since they spoke German and Polish, it was somewhat easier for them. But the risk they took was enormous.

From what we knew, the Poles in the countryside, like those in Auschwitz, were not friendly toward Jews.

At dawn, our pitiful column of men resumed its march. Although it was hard for us to carry on, the sight of our guards, themselves exhausted, gave us courage. At the end of those forty miles, having lost many men among our ranks, we arrived at a new camp. Gleiwitz had been partially emptied to make room for us. The sun had already set, and night engulfed the camp. We were lined up, and the SS began to inspect us. We were all too familiar with this routine and knew what it was about. They were examining us for selection. When they came to me, I was placed on one side in an enclosed barrack. Through the window, I saw the other barrack was open; the majority of the inmates were sent over there. My hour had come. There were no definite signs, but I was certain that they placed me with those they were planning to liquidate. I had no intention of letting myself be killed like this. My struggle had lasted for nearly a year, fighting to hold on, to survive, so that I would not get sucked down. All this for nothing? To die after struggling so hard and so long? What's more, the Soviets seemed very near. We could hear the sound of their guns in the distance. It was hardly the time to give in. I noticed the window was not latched. Taking advantage of the darkness, I pushed the window open, climbed through, walked around the barrack, and again took my place at the end of the line. I was panting hard. Living in the survival mode since my arrival in the camps meant that I was cut off from fear. But now it returned full force, gripping me, almost strangling me. The SS officer once again came up to me. He looked me over. I stood up as straight as I could. The cold and fatigue had left me. He sent me to the other barrack. I was going to live!

In reality, I never knew what was going on that night. Was it really a selection? I am not certain. But what I have retained from that night was the very distinct feeling that I had a close brush with death, one more time.

We had no respite. We were left in this camp, under surveillance, but abandoned, if you will, left to our own devices. We were not assigned to any block. We had to settle that by ourselves. It was freezing. We tried to go into the first barrack we saw, but noticed that it was already occupied. The inmates there had claimed space and would not let us in. We insisted that there was no room available elsewhere. The blows began to rain down. The inmates inside began to hit us when we opened the door. We did not try to force the issue, but not everyone was as willing to give in. In fact, others from our incoming group, exhausted from two days of walking, and freezing in this icy night, did try to force their way in. When they were hit, they hit back with whatever they could find. The camp was turned into an absolute hellhole; everybody was beating whomever they could with whatever they could find. Everybody was trying to hold on to or find a little bit of warmth and rest. This spectacle was unreal, unimaginably horrible. Cries, screams, insults, wails . . . insanity reigned. Meanwhile, the SS remained indifferent. There was no need for action on their part as the inmates were doing the work for them. Everywhere there were lifeless bodies, dead bodies, wounded bodies that would soon become corpses. We slept wherever we could, outside, warming each other as best we could, as far away as possible from those *häftlings* who had gone mad.

The next night we were ordered to march again. This time it was a short walk to a railroad. The Germans had managed, in spite of their impending downfall, to find us a train. The railroad cars were simply platforms with walls, but no roofs. We were ordered to climb in. We tried as best we could, but the climb was terribly hard.

Worse, we realized that more than one hundred of us were trying to get in the same car. This meant standing room only. We knew that we would all die if we traveled under these conditions. What happened then was once again harrowing. The insanity we had lived through the night before started anew. In order to sit down and have a little more space, a terrible fight broke out. The inmates were hitting each other with the intent to kill. It turned into a real slaughter. An abominable scene ensued, but survival was foremost. I was able to avoid the beating by taking refuge inside a square formed by my fellow Bobrek inmates. About twenty dead bodies were strewn beneath the living on the floor. It began to calm down. I was thirsty. My throat was dry from a fever. With my spoon, I scooped up some snow that was falling hard and accumulating on my friends' backs. They did the same. Then we all collapsed with fatigue on the corpses beneath us.

That terrible day, I was lucky not to have to fight. Moral concerns were not the thing that held me back. Morality had no place in this wretched world. If I had had to save my skin at the expense of another, I would have done so. But I knew that I could not have survived the blows. I did not have the strength anymore. The red triangle Poles who were striking freely were in much better health and much stronger than we were. The slightest blow would have been fatal for me; I did not have the strength to defend myself. I was totally worn out.

The locomotive whistle pierced the air and the train began its journey. In our car, we settled in for the trip, resting our bony buttocks on dead bodies instead of on the hard wooden floor that would have been unbearable. How long were we traveling? How many miles? None of us had any idea at the time. When we awoke, we were in the middle of a city, under a bridge, waiting for I don't know what. We knew we were in Prague, because it was written on a sign. We looked up at the bridge and noticed some people walking by. It was snowing hard. Someone stopped, leaned over the bridge and looked down at us. Then other people looked over as well. Soon, there was a whole group gazing down. All these heads covered with furry hats, wrapped in wooly scarves, looked at us, scrutinized us. We were silent, freezing, and cloaked in thin blankets, a bit ashamed of being examined in this way because we were so dirty and emaciated. Then suddenly, the group dissipated, all the heads disappeared. A few minutes went by. Then they all returned and shouted something to us that we did not understand. They tossed us bread, entire loaves of it. In fact their shouts were of encouragement. Then all went quiet. Emotions welled up in us. It was overwhelming. I had forgotten what a simple human gesture was. I had even forgotten that people could have relationships that were not based on a power struggle, that it was possible to give like this, that solidarity was not just an empty word. I shall never forget those citizens of Prague, nor will any of my companions. That day they gave us more than bread. At that moment, they gave us strength, the will to live, the will not to give up, to remain men, in spite of the fact that since Gleiwitz, we were almost dead and had virtually lost our humanity.

But that little glimmer of humanity did not make us forget the harsh reality that confronted us. For example, when we had to answer the call of nature, we had to alert our guards. Then we had to sit on the wall with our buttocks facing outside while the train was moving. At one point, we learned that the train was to stop and there would be a distribution of bread. An SS arrived, gun in hand, carrying a big sack. He motioned for all of us to move to his left and ordered each of us to take a loaf of bread, and then move off to his right. This orderly distribution allowed each of us to be served and avoided another scene of carnage. The train left once again. And we traveled for a long time. The following night we arrived in a new camp. Buchenwald.

From Buchenwald to Schwerin

I had been exhausted, completely discouraged, and on my last legs in the past, but for the first time now, I felt I could not go on. It was beyond my capacity. The tiny hope that I had been fostering until this point, that it would all finally come to an end, that I would escape from this nightmare, had vanished. I had had enough. I was beyond exhaustion. My body was burning. I was in pain. I did not see any way out. No way out but death. I was hoping in this new camp they would have gas chambers and that they would put an end to the wreck of a man that I had become.

But destiny would have things otherwise. We quickly learned that this new KZ (*konzentrationslager,* concentration camp) was not an extermination camp. It was not Birkenau. The inmates here, wearing striped outfits like us, some of them French and wearing the red triangles of political prisoners, were well aware of where we had come from and took us under their wing. They understood our desperation and wanted to reassure us: "Gather your friends. You have a chance to be saved here." It was the real shot in the arm I needed. Hope was rekindled in me despite the overwhelming fatigue.

The cold was glacial that moonless night. We walked through the barbed wire entrance, past the SS and their dogs. We entered a large wooden barrack where there were already many inmates who had made the journey with us. The clamor was deafening, but the animal warmth inside was a welcome change from outside.

We were served some warm soup, and then we each underwent an interrogation. It was clear that nobody had any background on us. The SS, who had to act hastily, did not send any documents ahead. I was asked my name, my "status," my job, and the *kommando* I belonged to. I took advantage of the confusion: I said I was a political prisoner, half-Jewish, *feinmechaniker,* from the Siemens *kommando.* As a Siemens worker, I might have a chance if Siemens existed here. And in becoming a political prisoner who was half-Jewish, I had a greater chance of survival than if I were 100 percent Jewish. I was assigned another number, but this time it was not tattooed on me.

I managed to find my friends from Bobrek, and we came together in the quarantine barracks where the inmates were held until they were assigned a new *kommando.*

The Buchenwald camp hierarchy was run mostly by red triangle political inmates, which allowed for a disciplinary regime that was less brutal than the green triangles imposed at Auschwitz. What's more, we discovered that our group fell within the jurisdiction of Marcel Paul, a French communist (who became part of the French government in 1946) running an underground operation within the camp organization. We were in luck, as it allowed us to survive without too much suffering. Thanks to them, information about the outside world trickled down to us. We learned of the advancing Soviet and American armies and of the extent of the debacle the German army was facing. Yet, Hitler seemed determined to fight until the bitter end. We were informed that France had been liberated and had been enjoying its freedom for several months. But we also knew that the SS were not about to loosen their grip on us.

Once again, fate came knocking. Siemens had found us and asked that we be transferred. We were informed that the move would take place in a few days.

While we waited, my nineteenth birthday came and went without my realizing it. Here, as in the other camps, there was nothing to help us determine the date or time. The only thing we could make out was day from night.

Albert Levy met up with a friend from his network in the French resistance. How sad to meet in such a place, but what a joy to find each other alive. According to his friend, the war was not going to last much longer. He advised Albert to remain at Buchenwald and not follow the Siemens *kommando*. He offered to "organize" a protected job for him. But Albert decided to entrust his destiny to our group from Bobrek.

In mid-February 1945, almost one year to the day after my expulsion from France, we found ourselves in two cattle cars attached to a freight train, heading in an unknown direction. Destination: a Siemens factory. This new "journey" had nothing in common with our last one, from Gleiwitz to Buchenwald. The car had a roof. There were only about fifty of us and we were among friends. The SS were traveling in a passenger car nearby. We could see just about everything that was happening outside through the small aperture.

Snow spread out as far as the eye could see. From time to time, we passed a train station. We chugged along at a slow pace. The locomotive whistle reminded me of the journey from Drancy to Auschwitz. The train would stop for hours on end, and we had no idea where we were going. At one point, we were in a large railroad station. We were unable to find out its name. It looked like a sprawling railway junction. Many trains went past slowly. The platform cars were packed tightly with enormous long-range guns and tanks. War materiel and equipment apparently were still plentiful. And there were still trains to move them around.

After a few days, we arrived in Berlin. We were taken underground where a subway car had been requisitioned for us alone. An air raid siren sounded, and hundreds of Berliners gathered on the platform. The sight of our group offered a rare spectacle. Standing there in front of our car, they were stunned to see prisoners wearing striped outfits, each more emaciated than the next, accompanied by their strapping healthy guards. Coming face to face with each other like this was staggering. The symbolism was irresistible. The master race, taking refuge in the bowels of its capital, was confronted with *untermenschen* (subhuman creatures) who were not yet annihilated.

Our subway car eventually took us to the suburbs of Berlin, where we arrived in a miniature camp modeled after Buchenwald. We were a few hundred yards from Siemensstadt, Siemens's industrial city.

The setting was the same . . . unchangeable. There were four or five barracks, and bunk beds with the same wooden slats that we would pile into like sardines to sleep. The food was the same as everywhere else, as bad as it was insufficient. And the factory was the same, as well as the work expected of us. The major difference between Bobrek and here was that we were not living on the factory grounds. The barracks were a bit farther away, in the center of town where we could witness the routines of daily life in the city. We, as slave laborers, worked at night when the Siemens factory workers, some of whom were French, were asleep. To keep us going during those night hours, they served us a "soup" that was nothing more than colored water with an occasional piece of rutabaga floating in it. It was absolutely revolting. Allied bombings often forced us to stop working and take cover in the cellars with the SS. One day, the bombing seemed to go on for longer than usual and it seemed very near us. The walls trembled and we had the feeling that trains were constantly running over our heads. When we finally left the cellars, we saw that everything was in ruins. It had all been reduced to a smoking rubble except for the building we worked in. So we went back to work. At dawn, when we returned to our camp, we found that everything had gone up in flames. As there was nowhere else to go, we remained outside under the surveillance of the SS. Since the "storage room" had been blown up, we found some raw potatoes on the ground and cooked them over the burning embers of the camp. For the first time in a long time, we felt we were really eating.

We obviously could not remain there and so we moved once again. The SS transferred us by truck to a new camp: Sachsenhausen, about twenty miles from Berlin. Once again, we had to go through registration and disinfection. This time I claimed to be an Aryan.

At Sachsenhausen, I was assigned to a *kommando* where I had to work outdoors. It was physically demanding. We had to clear away the rubble from the bombings. Once again, Siemens found us. We were dispatched, on those first days of April 1945, in a train heading for Bavaria, where another Siemens factory was waiting for us. However, we did not arrive there. We stopped at Dresden, blocked by the advancing Allied armies. One of the SS guards was happy to show us a newspaper that announced the death of U.S. president Franklin Roosevelt. Meanwhile the spectacle around us provided extraordinary consolation. The city had been bombed several weeks earlier. Nothing was left. What we saw for miles and miles, as far as the eye could see, was a town ravaged, razed to a pile of rocks and steel. We looked on the devastation with a smile that said much more than any words could have. I felt, as my companions did, an immense joy that was almost impossible to define and even more difficult to describe—a feeling perhaps of revenge and of the certitude that finally the end of this nightmare was in sight. For the first time in a very long time—too long—I almost felt lighthearted . . . happy.

Once again, however, reality caught up with us, forcing us out of our brief, joyful reverie. Blocked in Dresden, we had no other choice but to retrace our steps, and so we returned to Sachsenhausen. Once more we set to work clearing away the rubble, but this time in the streets of Berlin. Soldiers of fourteen and fifteen years old crossed our path, on the way to the front that no longer seemed very far off. The end was really near.

A few days later, we were assembled outside once again with a blanket and a loaf of bread, as in Bobrek. We began to march and were told we were heading for Lübeck. What would we be doing there? We were a bit anxious because Lübeck was a port city in the north of Germany. Were they planning to send us somewhere? What would the destination be? We marched for a long time. It was less cold, but it was similar to our march from Bobrek to Gleiwitz: the beatings, the gunshots, the dead left at the side of the road.

After a few days and nights of marching and sleeping outside, we came across the International Red Cross, whose absence had been, up until this point, quite conspicuous. While the SS looked on, people from the Red Cross distributed packages containing chocolate, margarine, and all sorts of things that should never be given to people suffering from malnutrition. We pounced on this food, which we had not seen for months, even years.

The following day, May 3, 1945, we awoke at dawn in the woods of Crivitz and noticed that our guards had disappeared. What we did see were men on horseback. The Red Army. We were finally free. The nightmare had ended. Without even a second thought, almost spontaneously, we all broke out into a chorus of "L'Internationale." One of the soldiers invited us to "return to our homes": "*Domoi.*" We were more than anxious to do so. But which way? We had no idea where we were or what road to take to return

home. We walked for several hours, taking the road before us, and
arrived in a small town, Schwerin. My friend, Bernard Kuhl, and I
entered a large abandoned house. On the second floor, we found
rooms everywhere with big beds that looked very comfortable. We
went to sleep, each in his own room. But we were too excited to
sleep . . . too excited and too sick. In fact, the food the Red Cross
had distributed provoked terrible stomach pains and uncontrollable
diarrhea. Holding it in was impossible. And each time we had an
accident, we would laugh a lot. Then we would go into another
room and slip into a clean bed that we would soon dirty again. We
were like kids, playing at this little game that caused us much pleasure. We were truly drunk with the freedom that had finally come
to us . . . freedom that we had stopped believing in. A short while
later, we went into the back of a grocer's shop and discovered a barrel of powdered chocolate. We literally pounced on it and stuffed
ourselves.

That was the only revenge we took on Germany and the
Germans. We never thought about avenging ourselves in any other
way on those who had plunged us into hell. We were too happy to
be free. Free and alive.

Paris

From Schwerin, in the Soviet zone, we passed into the British zone, where the English authorities, who did not seem to understand what we had been through, placed us in a military barracks named Adolf Hitler. They were very cold and treated us harshly, as if we were criminals. Dressed in civilian clothes, we then moved into the American zone. Little by little, I lost my companions who departed for their respective homes one after another. So it was alone, with other former deported men and women I did not know, that I took the train for Paris several days later.

In Paris, on May 23, 1945, a welcoming committee greeted us. We were taken to the Hotel Lutetia on the Left Bank where I, like everyone else, was submitted to an interview. When was I arrested? When was I deported? Which camps had I been to? Some file cards were put together by the French authorities to verify the information during the interview. A few years ago, I found these cards about me in the National Archives along with those about my parents.

I was officially a racial deportee—the title would soon be modified to read "political deportee." For a few days, I had a room at the Hotel Lutetia. The cushiony bed was extraordinary. The clean sheets enveloped in a billowy comforter were so soft in comparison to the rough blanket we had in the camp. I felt as if I were floating in a cloud. In a few days, I rediscovered sensations that I had forgotten: comfort, pleasure. And my agonized body was slowly becoming unknotted. I began to fortify myself, eating until I was satiated, drinking until my thirst was quenched, and watching the deep wound on my left foot from my wooden shoe finally begin to heal. My libido began to stir. It had remained dormant when I was in the camp. I never thought about sex at all when I was an inmate because I never felt any urges. When a body is sick, starving, and thirsty, it has no desires. Preoccupied with surviving, eating, drinking, concerned with self-preservation, a body in this condition has no desires. But here in my cushiony bed, in the warmth of the room where I could forget it all, I began to live again, to have sensations, feelings, desires. At the Hotel Lutetia, I met a charming young woman who was assigned to help me get settled in at the Hotel Rothschild on Avenue de Marignan (near the presidential palace on the Right Bank) where I was sent for several days. I spent the first night with her there, and what a marvelous night it was. She knew who I was, what I had lived through, and without a word, she got undressed and came into my bed. She let me warm my emaciated body of a hundred pounds against her body. All night, she offered me warmth, tenderness, and comfort without any expectations.

Meanwhile, I returned to rue Geoffroy l'Angevin, where the concierge told me that our apartment had been held for us by the manager of the building. Mr. Moeneclay was an admirable man who did not profit from the situation. What a shock to return to this apartment where I had lived so happily with my parents. It was empty. There was no furniture, not even a scrap of paper. Well actually, there was one sheet of paper on the floor—the notice that sealed the apartment. I kept it. The concierge had been there when the contents of the apartment were taken away, as she told me in all seriousness, by the "authorities."

I went to visit my mother's cousin, Mayer Elina. I learned that he, his wife, Georgette, and their son, Jean, had also been deported and had not returned. My mother's brother, Albert, who had been taken as a POW, had just returned to Paris. The family, or what was left of it, got together at the home of Henri, Mayer's brother, who was designated as my guardian.

Since I had to earn a living, I went back to work at Caudron. It was as if I had never left. My job had been held for me as the apartment had been held for me. I had the same address, the same apartment, the same job, the same hours. I took the same subway to get to the same office and saw the same colleagues. Life continued as if nothing at all had happened.

In my apartment, there was only one sofa, which my guardian had given me, and I had purchased a bed. The familiar objects were no longer there. The presence of my parents, so connected to this apartment, with all those strong memories, haunted me. They would not be coming back. I suffered in the realization that nothing of them remained, except the precious contents of the suitcase that the Culets had returned to me. I suffered because I would not be able to go to their graves and properly mourn their loss. The first questions began to surface. It was unbearable. How . . . Why had this all happened?

I could not forget the beatings, the cold, the hunger, the corpses, the smokestacks, and the odor. I could not forget the camps and that arrival in Auschwitz, the first conversations with the inmate, the march to Gleiwitz, the insanity of that camp, the train and the march to Lübeck. The omnipresent images were ingrained. I could not chase them away. They were images in which I appeared. Nothing could ever be as it was before. But I wanted to forget it all. Forget that I was there, that my parents died there, and that friends I made had died there too. I never spoke about my experiences. Not with anyone. Not even with my childhood friends with whom I was reunited in Paris, Maxime Doukhan and Henri Tchervinsky. They sensed it all, but asked nothing. I knew, but I could not say anything. We never spoke of it, yet all of our conversations were tinged with the experiences that I had been lucky enough to escape. We would stay up nights on end talking, not about how to change the world, but about how we could live in it. Where could we go and live happily and peacefully? Shouldn't we have a place that was our own, a place where we would be sure that we would not be harassed for what we were? Palestine! But what if we wanted to stay where we were? We came to the conclusion that we could no longer be what we were, or more precisely, that we would have to make others forget that we were Jews. When I was going from camp to camp, I lost a little of my identity each time: Jewish, half-Jewish, not Jewish at all. It was my way of protecting myself and of course somewhat softening the conditions that I had to face. From a strictly personal point of view, it was also a way of hiding something in me that the others would never be ready to accept. This was not some sort of self-hatred, but simply a method of self-preservation and of escaping the barbarism if it were to ever break out again.

So I did not talk about it. I wanted to live peacefully and not risk being plunged back into the horror that I had experienced. When I returned to work at Caudron, I asked that my name be spelled differently: Michelin, inserting an *e* so I could forget.

That lasted only a few weeks. I quickly understood that it would not change anything and that one must live inside oneself and not be concerned about what others think. I went back to the original spelling of Michlin. I was Jewish and would remain so whether people liked it or not.

Perhaps the best way of forgetting was to go away, embark on a new life and leave behind this one that was increasingly difficult for me to bear in this country. But where to go? Palestine, as Henri, Maxime, and I discussed, did not attract me. The idea of spending my life at Caudron hardly excited me. Be an actor? In fact, soon after my return to Paris, I auditioned for a part using the Molière monologue that had been so successful at Bobrek. I was not selected. In the end, I was not willing to work in such a risky field. I dreamed of studying again. But where? Why not go to the United States, where I had family who would welcome me? Morris Wainger, my father's cousin, to whom I had been writing for some time, proposed that I come. He had sent over two cousins who had participated in the D-Day landings to see what had become of us. I answered him that if there was a chance that I could study, I was ready to come immediately. In the weeks that followed, we spoke of nothing but this project, considering the financial angles, my age, etc. We talked about how a man, twenty years old, like myself, could adapt to this new environment. As a last resort, Morris Wainger asked me to see one of his friends, a lawyer in Paris, to "size me up." My enthusiasm, my determination to start anew, and my strong desire to leave the France that had permitted what had happened to me and allowed my parents to die abominably—in spite of their devotion to the country—made it clear that I was intent on leaving. We quickly started drawing up the papers that would allow me to emigrate.

Meanwhile, I was traveling a little. Caudron gave me a few weeks off so I could recover. I was still very thin and frail at this point, so I went for a rest to Grenoble, in the French Alps, where my friends Félix Russac and Jacquot lived. Félix, after participating in the Underground in Vercors, was selling thread in the market. Jacquot was being treated in a sanatorium in Saint-Hilaire du Touvet. They had escaped the atrocities.

I stayed in Grenoble for a couple of weeks, close to them, and then returned to Paris. I went back to the factory convinced a little more each day that I needed a change in my life. I was impatient for my papers to be ready so that I could start living my new life in America.

In a few weeks, thanks to the influence and the hard work of Morris Wainger, everything was ready: the affidavit, the permanent visa from the American embassy, the exit visa from France, and a ticket on the ship *La Désirade,* a fortuitous name. Prohibited from exporting money, I gathered all my possessions and sold the little furniture I owned. With that money I had my friend Henri's parents make a nice ring for me with my initials on it. I gave my notice at Caudron and patiently awaited the date of my departure. My girlfriend, whom I met at the factory, did everything in her power to keep me from leaving. She even feigned pregnancy and insisted that I had to stay. My neighbor on rue Geoffroy l'Angevin, the cobbler, who had been lucky enough to escape the roundups, also tried to discourage me from leaving. He wanted me to marry his daughter. But I knew what I wanted and especially what I did not want. I did not want to work at Caudron anymore. I did not want a job I did not like, nor to have to deal with my colleagues who were harder and harder to bear. As time went on, I was getting the feeling they reproached me for having survived the camp and come back. I never spoke of my experiences. They had lived through the Occupation, mostly indifferent to what had gone on and at times seemed to have approved it. They would ask the most tactless questions that made me nervous and were hurtful. It almost felt as though they suspected me of making up stories. "How were you able to return, if everybody else died?"

I was fed up with France. Nothing had been resolved. The national reconstruction, the famous national reconciliation meant that everyone in the administration remained in place. When I returned from the camps, I went to the police precinct where my mother and I had been arrested and held before being sent to Drancy. I wanted to see the police officers who had come to our apartment that infamous night to arrest us. Vengeance was not my motivation. I just wanted to tell them what my life had been like after they had so conscientiously fulfilled their duty and what had happened to my mother. The authorities were less than accommodating and would not provide the officers' names. That period was over, forgotten. It was another time, another era. Even today, the police *préfecture* pretends not to understand what it had actively participated in. They do not wish to understand; it seems of little concern to them. A simple visit to the extensive exhibition held for the bicentennial of the police *préfecture* in 1994 was convincing enough on this point. The exhibition emphasized the few days involved in the Liberation of Paris and the heroic conduct of a few; it remained virtually silent on the active and zealous collaboration of so many during the four-year German Occupation.

As I write this today, I can console myself with President Jacques Chirac's declaration of July 16, 1995, on the occasion of the fifty-third anniversary of the Vélodrome d'Hiver roundup, calling on France to face its painful history of the wartime period. But I cannot help thinking about the declarations made on several occasions during François Mitterrand's presidency from 1981 through May 1995. Refusing to take a stand on the German Occupation, Mitterrand hid behind the most elegant arguments. He claimed that the French state at that time was not France. Therefore the president of the republic today, being the highest authority of the state, did not have to ask forgiveness or even provide an explanation (consciously ignoring the fact that he himself had participated in the Vichy government) for the behavior of the Vichy government officials who had strayed from the republic and disdained its values.

All the government employees who had signed arrest orders, police officers who implemented them without any compunction, railroad workers who transported people to their deaths, all carried on their lives after the war without even a second thought. I was ashamed of this country that refused to face up to its past, and I knew that the anti-Semitism that had promoted these infamous laws was not dead.

For all of these reasons, leaving became imperative.

While I waited those few weeks, I kept busy. My friend Guy Lohac,knew a lot of people, and we often spent our nights at the well-known Lido nightclub backstage watching from the wings. We came up with some fantastic projects. As the salesman for Bordeaux wines, he wanted me to be his exclusive representative in America. The project was too ambitious for me. I simply wanted to be a student.

The night before my departure, at the start of the evening at the Lido, we decided to take advantage of our last evening together. We did not know if we would ever see each other again. As we had met two nice young ladies, we decided to go to a hotel that Guy knew, where we took two adjoining rooms. It was an extraordinary night in which our imaginations burst out in ways we had barely suspected. And the next morning, very early, completely exhausted, Guy accompanied me to the Saint Lazare train station where I was to take the train to Le Havre. I was a little sad to say good-bye to him. But France was already far away. I did not miss it at all. I left on April 12, 1946, happy, ready for the discovery of America.

Epilogue

The United States was an incredible experience for me. It changed my life entirely. My family was warm and welcoming, and I experienced the practices of Judaism for the first time. I was completely immersed in the English language. I entered the university, a place where democratic principles played themselves out, a place where freedom of expression was exhilarating, and where I discovered people could have mutual respect for one another. It all felt like a new world.

I received my diploma as a mathematical engineer. I worked as an actuary in an insurance company, as a mechanical engineer in an aviation factory, then as a development engineer in a carburetor factory. Then one day, before the birth of electronic data processing, IBM offered me an international career that has continued to fascinate me, especially since I had anticipated the explosive growth of the computer. The experience took me to Rome, twice to New York, and then three separate times to Paris, where I was named European director of telecom products in 1980.

I never thought I would return to Paris. It was a great joy to find myself in the city where I had grown up. I met up again with my friends: Jacquot, Maurice, Guy, and Henri. I went to my old neighborhood, rue Rambuteau, and the playgrounds where my mother took me to play as a child, the schools where I had received my early education.

It was a shock to find myself in these familiar settings. And even years later, it was still painful. Emotions would well up when I went to these places. Things had changed. The rue Rambuteau had lost its vegetable carts. Art galleries had mushroomed up, replacing the little stalls, and the open space at Beaubourg had become the Pompidou Center. Still, something in the air remained unchanged. I could not visit this neighborhood without nostalgia and great emotion. The rue Geoffroy l'Angevin was still there with its history, our history. My heart would tighten, a knot forming in my throat. My parents' memory haunts these streets, these buildings.

In this same neighborhood, a few blocks away on rue Geoffroy l'Asnier, now stands the CDJC, the Center for Contemporary Jewish Documentation, with its sober memorial dedicated to those Jews who disappeared. It is just a few hundred yards from the police precinct from which the police officers were sent out to arrest us, the cursed police precinct with the marble plaque whose text still remains incomplete.

Perhaps today I am finally accepted for what I am. But I have not forgotten, and I shall never forget that I and my parents, who lost their lives because of it, were of no interest to the nation.

SOURCES FOR RESEARCH

Archives Départementales de la Gironde, Bordeaux.

Archives Nationales, Ministère de la Culture, Paris.

Centre des Archives Contemporaines, Ministère de la Culture, Fontaine-
bleau.

Centre de Documentation Juive Contemporaine (CDJC), Paris.

Klarsfeld, Serge. *Le mémorial de la déportation des juifs de France.* Paris:
Klarsfeld, 1978.

U.S. Immigration and Naturalization Service, Department of Justice, New
York, N.Y.

U.S. National Archives and Records Administration, New York, N.Y.

Yad Vashem, The Holocaust Martyrs' and Heroes' Remembrance Authority, Jerusalem.

YIVO Institute for Jewish Research, New York, N.Y.

AFTERWORD:
THE WAR AGAINST THE ENLIGHTENMENT
AND AGAINST THE JEWS
Zeev Sternhell

Gilbert Michlin's narrative grips the reader from beginning to end. Were it not for the hell that looms out of his pages, one might almost say that his strikingly sober and austere account has many of the characteristic features of a genuine work of imaginative literature. But in reconstructing his Parisian microcosm, Michlin does not intend to do the work of a creative writer. Sixty years after the events, after searching his memory and consulting the historical archives, he has given us an exemplary case study that sheds light on the fate of ordinary Jews, modest people without wealth, connections, or resourcefulness, with no courageous Christian friends, and thus lacking the lucky star that allowed others to survive.

After World War I, the majority of the Jewish people were still living in Eastern Europe, divided between the Soviet Union and the newly independent states that arose from the dismemberment of the old multinational empires. Established on the basis of nationalities, these new states, Poland in particular, had a strong aversion to minorities. The postwar states of Eastern Europe continued the imperial trend of casting out the Jews begun in the 1880s and forced hundreds of thousands more to seek refuge in the 1920s. At that very moment, America closed its gates and never again opened them to free immigration, not at any time and not for any reason.

Gilbert Michlin was born in Paris by chance. If his father, Moshe Michlin, had landed in New York a few months earlier, before the new immigration policy was put in place, he might not have been turned back from Ellis Island in November 1923, and Gilbert might have been born in Detroit, where two of Moshe's brothers were living. But this Russian-speaking Jew from Lachowicz, in the northeastern part of interwar Poland, close to

Lithuania and Belarus, came before the Statue of Liberty at a moment when white, Protestant America was in one of the periodic waves of patriotic hysteria that recurred throughout the twentieth century. In the name of defending "American values," there was an explosion of strong animosity toward foreigners, frequently Jews, as well as against blacks, "leftists," and other "undesirables." Gilbert's father thus learned that anti-Semitism was not the exclusive characteristic of Poles, Russians, and Ukrainians.

Born in Montmartre on February 5, 1926, and raised in the Paris neighborhoods of Les Halles, Le Marais, and La Bastille, Gilbert Michlin, computer specialist, former director of IBM telecommunications products for Europe, is now a United States citizen. On his return from deportation to the concentration camps, he decided to cut ties with France. As a Polish Jew born in France, Gilbert Michlin confirms the rule: many of those who survived the Shoah could no longer breathe in Europe. But as a "French Jew," this child of Paris is an extremely rare case: French Jews who left the country after the war can be counted on one's fingers.

Alone upon his return from deportation, Michlin lived in his family's apartment in Paris, emptied of its contents but reserved for him by the building manager awaiting the possible return of its tenants. Michlin resumed work at the Caudron company, utilizing the skills of a toolmaker that had enabled him to survive as a slave of Siemens at Birkenau, but he was so uncomfortable that he felt compelled to leave. He would succeed where his father had failed; he would become an American. For this young man who had seen his mother, Riwka Dworetzkaia, marching to the gas chamber, France would forever bear the responsibility for the death of his parents and the horror that he lived through.

Gilbert Michlin set out for the New World in early 1946 not only because he had family there. He also had a cousin and an aunt in Palestine, where the long war for independence had already begun. Riwka Dworetskaia's sister was one of the founding members of the Messilot kibbutz, at the foot of Mount Gilboa, in the heart of the beautiful agricultural land in the north of the country that had become the symbol of Jewish national rebirth. Her relatives could have joined her; if the Michlins or the Michlens (the spelling varies) had turned to Palestine instead of trying to gain entry to the United States, they would have taken their place among the founders of Israel. As members of a kibbutz, they could have belonged to the celebrated pioneer elite that built, at least in the confines of a collective agricultural settlement, not only a nation but also a new society. But, in fact, Gilbert Michlin's parents, like himself a quarter century later, were not from the stock of pioneers and builders. Like most East European Jews, they professed no strong convictions and did not belong to an activist minority.

The Michlins were not Zionists, and they were not Communists. Nor were they Bundists, that is, non-Zionist Jewish socialists, who were Yiddish-speaking revolutionary internationalists loyal to the Jewish national and cultural heritage, people convinced that the fate of the Jews was tied to the emancipation of the proletariat. The Michlins did not think about Jewish identity, the establishment of a nation, or world revolution; they wanted only to live untroubled like their family in America, whose example they had before them. They were ordinary Jews dreaming of a world in which they could have a place, however modest, of a life without virulent anti-Semitism that was too harsh or too flagrant, a life to which they no longer dared aspire in their native country. There were 2.4 million Jews like Moshe and Riwka Michlin who left Eastern Europe between the great czarist pogroms of the 1880s and 1924, the year of the new American immigration laws. Among them, only 40,000 to 50,000 landed on the shores of Palestine, which became a country of immigrants only when there was really nowhere else to go, as in the interwar period when nearly 340,000 immigrants came, chiefly from Poland and Germany.

Driven to emigrate by poverty as much as by the hatred of Jews that flourished on the eastern borders of Poland perhaps more than any other region of the world, the Michlins still had somewhere to go. Riwka Michlin was a French teacher, for the time an emancipated and culturally assimilated young woman. She dreamed of Paris, where she already had a brother and a cousin who owned a hat factory. Her husband, Moshe, who was a Hebrew teacher and probably also a *melamed* (teacher in a Jewish religious school), would become a cutter in the hat factory, a preeminently Jewish occupation. The necessity of fleeing independent Poland was such that this intellectual, who had never worked with his hands, agreed to become a common laborer.

From their very first days in Paris, the integration of this young immigrant family followed a peaceful, almost linear pattern. "Life was beautiful," says Gilbert Michlin of his childhood. Certainly, compared to the anti-Semitic and poor Polish country-side still barely touched by modernization, France was a dream country. Overcome by gratitude for the country that received them, the young couple played the game of assimilation whole-heartedly. So that nothing would distinguish the newcomers from their surroundings, they even changed their names: Moshe became Maurice and Riwka, Renée. Her brother, Avram, now Albert, with a non-Jewish girlfriend, had already shown the way. By pure chance, their family name, very common in Slavic countries (in Prague, for example, there is a Mechlen neighborhood), when pronounced in French brought to mind not only the famous tire maker, but could have been considered one of the numerous deriv-atives of Michel.

The Michlins were not religious and did not belong to a synagogue. They read *L'Œuvre* but were not active in any of the numerous left-wing organizations, notably the Communist organi-zations that were particularly hospitable to foreigners. It goes with-out saying that they did not do battle in the great political demon-strations of these troubled years. In short, they did everything they could to melt into the great mass of ordinary people, respecting order, working hard, and being content with their lot. Moshe and Riwka's only son was named Gilbert, Gigi to his mother. He was circumcised, but he never fasted on Yom Kippur, and he did not become a bar mitzvah. Of course, he also had a Hebrew name, Solomon, with the Yiddish diminutive "Zalmonke," but it was used only by the immediate family and only in his early childhood. Although he was the son of a former schoolteacher who earned his living in Poland by teaching Hebrew, he did not learn that lan-guage. And although Gilbert understood Yiddish and could appre-ciate the classic Jewish humor of Sholem Aleichem, he did not speak Yiddish.

The absence of Yiddish is a good indication of the atmosphere of the family setting and of the spirit in which the integration of this immigrant family into society took place. Michlin gives a detailed account of his Sundays, but he does not utter a word about Saturday, the Sabbath; his silences, as instructive as his fascinating narrative, are an integral part of the text. We can guess that Saturday was a normal work day, he at school, his father at the workshop. It goes without saying that the hat factory of cousin Mayer Elina (Yellin), like any other business, was closed on Sunday. For little Gilbert, this was the great day of the week. Shabbat did not exist, not even for a few minutes at nightfall, and Riwka Michlin did not light the Friday night Sabbath candles, the traditional role for the Jewish mother, almost sacred for women of that generation. In America, where public school children also went to classes on Saturday and men went to work, the majority of first-generation immigrant Jews, even if they were secular, were intent on maintaining a minimum of Jewish identity. This was not true for the Michlins; apart from enjoying the Yiddish theater troupe visiting from New York, Gilbert remembers chiefly traditional Jewish cooking: *gefilte fish, latkes, knaidlach.*

While his parents occasionally allowed themselves a nostalgic moment—a Soviet film in Russian, which recalled not only their first language of culture but also familiar landscapes—the child was French to his fingertips. This intelligent boy, first in his class, passionately interested in math, was lucky enough to have splendid parents. His father devoted Sunday, his only day off, to him; his cultivated mother, who spoke several languages, was a constant and decisive presence. Michlin does not say as much, but his parents seem to have lived principally for their only son. His attachment to their memory, the boundless love that he still bears toward the mother who vanished before his eyes, are rooted in the feeling that he was everything that counted for them in their life. When the neighborhood police came to get them (his father was already gone), Gilbert refused to run away, even though he could easily have taken advantage of an opportunity to do so, in order not to abandon his mother. He returned to take his place by her side in the police station on Place Baudoyer in the 4th arrondissement, and left with her for the Drancy transit camp.

Like all Jewish mothers, Renée Michlin dreamed of making her son into a doctor. Gilbert wanted to be an actor. In the end, despite his intellectual qualities and success in school, his academic and character prizes, he became a toolmaker. Having learned from experience, Maurice Michlin wanted his son to have a skill, a usable one, wanted him to know how to do something with his hands. This is why he refused to have him continue an academic education, and why, after elementary school, he chose for Gilbert the Dorian technical school. (It was only later in the United States that this gifted tool-and-die maker became an engineer.) Specializing in aeronautics, after three years of intensive study, Michlin went to work at the Caudron airplane factory in Boulogne-Billancourt. This was in August 1942, and the war against the Jews was in full swing.

It is worth summarizing a few essential facts here. On the eve of the Holocaust, out of a population of 43 million, France had between 300,000 and 330,000 Jews, approximately 90,000 of whom were "French Israelites" of old stock.[1] With a total population that counted 15 million more people than Poland, France had a Jewish population that was one-tenth the size. Immigrants from Eastern and Central Europe had come in three successive waves. The first followed the Russian pogroms of the 1880s; the second, including the Michlins, brought fugitives from the countries that had attained independence at the end of World War I; and the third followed the rise of Nazism. In all, the Jews never represented more than 0.8 percent of the French population. These figures alone justify some puzzlement about the existence of a "Jewish Question" in a country like France. For although there might have been a problem in Poland, where Jews made up about 9.5 percent of the population (30 percent in the major industrial centers of Warsaw and Łódz, and countless villages with majority or totally Jewish populations), and while most Polish Jews could be "accused" of still speaking Yiddish, and while it could be held against the Jews of Galicia that they were drawn toward Vienna and still yearned for the gentle paternalism of the old Emperor Franz-Joseph, nothing of this kind existed in France.

In France, the country of the Enlightenment, the Revolution, and the Rights of Man, Jews, loyal and extremely patriotic citizens, had only one real aspiration: to blend into the nation. During World War I, whether they were French or foreign, Jews had behaved impeccably, even in the eyes of the most convinced anti-Semites. It was Maurice Barrès, the living symbol of nationalism and anti-Semitism, who memorialized the death of the chief rabbi of Lyon, Abraham Bloch, who was killed in September 1914. According to legend, the rabbi, who was serving as chaplain to the Fourteenth Army Corps at the Battle of the Marne, was killed by a shell immediately after having given a Catholic soldier a crucifix to kiss. This exploit, real or imaginary, was exalted by Barrès, the author of *Les Déracinés* (The Uprooted), in one of his articles on "the spiritual families of France,"[2] and thoroughly exploited by him, whom *Le Canard enchaîné* crowned as the second greatest brain-washer in France.[3] Bloch's death occurred at a crucial moment in national history, recounted by a press that had still been violently anti-Semitic a few weeks earlier, and became one of the symbols of the *Union sacrée* as well as a kind of collective calling card for the Jews of France. It was therefore not surprising that fewer than 2 percent of school-age Jewish children were attending a Yiddish or a traditional religious school.

In Poland, on the other hand, an intense, autonomous Jewish cultural life was flourishing, both in Yiddish, the language of the people, and in Hebrew, the language of the nationalist elite. The great majority of primary-school pupils were registered in schools that in varying degrees presented themselves as Jewish, religious or secular, if only by closing on Saturday. In Jewish high schools (quality secondary education in Warsaw was open to very few Jews), Hebrew was written and spoken with the same facility as in Tel Aviv. In every major Polish city, political parties and youth movements were preparing groups of active members for a life as pioneers in the emerging Jewish homeland. On the eve of the catastrophe, tens of thousands of the members of Zionist youth groups were waiting for their *certificate,* their visa for Palestine, which Great Britain had just closed to Jewish immigration.[4] Between the wars, Poland was the scene of the struggle for power within the world Zionist movement. For nearly six months in 1934, David Ben Gurion conducted his electoral campaign there for the Zionist Congress, the parliament of the Jewish national movement. Following his victory in Poland, the head of the Labor Party took over leadership of the Zionist movement and became president of the Jewish Agency. In that capacity, Ben Gurion was to lead the Jews of Palestine to independence. This was the reality: the Jews of Poland, like their Ukrainian and German counterparts, were a national minority that declared itself and was represented as such in the Warsaw Parliament.

Is there any basis for a comparison with France? We have already seen the desire for integration on the part of Riwka-Renée and Moshe-Maurice, their determination to erase whatever might distinguish them. And yet, their request for naturalization, presented in 1933, was finally and definitively rejected on June 2, 1939. The campaign against foreigners was then at its height, and Charles Maurras, the leading anti-Semite, was elected that year to the Académie Française. Once again, Moshe, now Maurice, Michlin, who had already been turned back from New York, touched bottom. In October 1933, the police commissioner of the quartier Saint-Merri had explained his decision in these terms: *The present request is of no interest to the Nation.*

Indeed, what interest could there be in the intention of a Jewish hat worker to accede to French citizenship at a time when a furious campaign had been unleashed in the right-wing press, which dominated a large segment of public opinion, against a possible invitation to Albert Einstein to speak to the Collège de France? It is probable that Einstein's presence in Paris and even his naturalization might draw some positive national interest. But clearly, since the late nineteenth-century campaigns against foreigners, since Boulangism (that monarchist, anti-republican movement), and the Dreyfus Affair, the Jewish Question in France had not been discussed with reference to concrete practices but rather as a matter of principle. That is why it was laughable to consider the merits of one person or another; for the entire substantial layer of opinion makers for whom anti-Semitism was a pillar of national identity, the question of usefulness did not even arise. Besides, even had it been achieved, the Michlins' belated naturalization would, from the summer of 1940 on, in no way have changed the situation of the family. As the vise closed, the Jews were alone, more than they had ever been since the beginnings of modern anti-Semitism.

In the same vein, the essential question was not to determine whether the Jewish hat worker was worthy of a place under the common roof because of exceptional services in the past. It is certain that Moshe-Maurice Michlin had not distinguished himself more than Paul-Louis Weiller, a decorated pilot and commander of the Legion of Honor, who had received twelve medals during World War I. Major Weiller, who was wounded in the throat in the course of one air battle, thereafter suffered a fractured skull when his plane crashed. Decorated by both Marshal Joffre and Marshal Pétain, he was stripped of French citizenship on November 1, 1940.[5] A century and a half after the emancipation of the Jews by the French Revolution, Weiller's status was not very different from that of a Polish Jew who had arrived in France toward the end of 1924. A truly symbolic case was recorded in North Africa: just as the law of October 7, 1940, revoking the Crémieux decree[6] entered into force, Lieutenant Amar was posthumously awarded the Military Medal and the Legion of Honor for his feats of arms at the battle of the Aisne in June 1940.[7] Amar, a Jew, thus simultaneously received a high military distinction and posthumously lost his French citizenship.

Examples were countless. They include the councillor of state Jacques Helbronner, a colonel in the reserves, commander of the Legion of Honor, recipient of the Croix de Guerre 1914-1918, and the deputy Pierre Masse, who had fought at Verdun, both descendants of old "Israélite" families. They had been connected to Marshal Pétain since the Great War, one having served in the office of the minister of war and the other having sat with Pétain on the war committee; both died in the camps just like Moshe-Maurice

Michlin. As for Riwka-Renée Michlin, could a Polish Jew expect a different fate from the one that awaited Béatrice Reinach (née Camondo), sister of a war hero who had fallen in battle in 1917 and daughter-in-law of an illustrious scientist? On November 20, 1943, Béatrice and Léon Reinach, along with their children Fanny and Bertrand, joined twelve hundred other Jews in convoy 62 to Auschwitz. Two months later, on January 20, 1944, in convoy 66, it was Moshe Michlin's turn. Riwka and her son left on February 10, with convoy 68, not knowing that Moshe had gone before them. A few days earlier, on February 5, Gilbert had turned eighteen.

Gilbert Michlin's parents, like six million of their fellows, have no gravesite other than group monuments. The same thing is not true for a great family of the Parisian aristocracy, patrons of the arts, the family of the Counts of Camondo. In the chapel above the family tomb, a plaque was engraved in memory of the four members of the family who were deported, like the Michlins, interned in Drancy and sent to the east a few weeks before them. The inscription on the plaque is worth noting: "Died for France in 1943 and 1944." Another family member, Nissim Camondo, Béatrice's older brother, was a monoplane pilot and aerial observer, with several medals from the army, who died in battle on September 3, 1917, having shot down the enemy plane that had attacked him on his reconnaissance mission. But, whereas Air Lieutenant Camondo, a "prime example of the French officer, had died for France," as *Le Figaro* wrote on the occasion of his sumptuous funeral, his sister and her family "had died *by* France."[8] This expression from author Pierre Assouline, literally and figuratively, provides the central theme of Gilbert Michlin's narrative.

The Vichy government's anti-Jewish policy was of such importance that it was applied without exception. For the new regime, the soul and the spirit of the nation were at stake. This is why Marshal Pétain, the hero of Verdun, did nothing for his companions in arms. Solidarity based on milieu, class, or career, and even the deepest solidarity between men who had risked their lives on the same battlefields for the same cause, fell apart in the face of the demands of the National Revolution. Almost the entirety of the elite identified with "the work of national rebirth" undertaken by Pétain. Seventeen Jewish members of the Conseil d'État were removed, and this major institution of the republican state expressed not the slightest regret. In fact, the Conseil d'État applied the anti-Jewish policy rigorously, even passionately. The same thing was true for the Bar Association, the Collège de France, universities and *lycées,* and, in general, for the administration as a whole.

The position of the French Catholic Church at the time was of prime importance. With a few exceptions (including the archbishop of Toulouse and the bishop of Montauban, authors of powerful and well-known critiques, and the Jesuit Father Gaston Fessard, author of the famous manifesto *France, beware of losing thy soul*), the Church ardently supported Pétain and accepted the anti-Jewish policy without a trace of protest. Cardinal Baudrillart, for example, was a signatory in 1935 to the manifesto of Henri Massis, *Pour la défense de l'Occident,* justifying the Italian invasion of Ethiopia in the name of the higher values of civilization. He also was a member of the honorary committee of the collaboration group. When the Germans attacked the Soviet Union in June 1941, this prince of the church, "priest and Frenchman," who was then rector of the Institut Catholique de Paris, hailed the "age of a new crusade. I declare that the tomb of Christ will be delivered. . . . The Christian and civilized world is rising up with formidable strength to defend and save our Christian civilization."[9] The idea of a crusade against bolshevism was commonplace: in July, Emmanuel Mounier, intellectual leader of the Catholic "left," referring to communism, expressed the hope that it would finally be possible to "sterilize with a branding iron the political and social wound that it has created on the weakened body of Europe,"[10] for there was "no one who is not ready to hail the fall of the dark Stalinist regime on the day that it happens, as a deliverance for Europe, as long as it is not followed by similarly evil consequences. Among the faces of the Antichrist, the face of the cunning, vain, and bloody petty tyrant who has for years cut off Europe from Holy Russia and from all the powers of the new Russia, has been one of the most odious."[11] The war against atheistic communism obviously hinged on the re-Christianization of

France. For many ordinary people who accepted both traditional Catholic anti-Semitism and the anti-Semitism of Action Française (a nationalist and royalist movement), the elevation of the war against the Soviet Union to the status of a crusade could not fail to weaken the possibility of opposition to Vichy policies, thereby making the situation of the Jews even more precarious.

Cardinal Baudrillart was an extreme case, but he was not unique. Like him, Cardinals Gerlier, Suhard, and Liénart were concerned with the interests of the Church, the question of religious education, the fear of communism—in short with the "re-Christianization" of France. The position of Cardinal Suhard, archbishop of Paris, was more ambiguous than that of Cardinal Baudrillart, but he was not opposed to an understanding with the German occupation forces. With respect to the new regime and the person of the head of state, the position of the hierarchy was perfectly clear: "We venerate the head of state, and we earnestly ask that the entire French population unite around him," proclaimed a July 1941 declaration published by the assembly of French bishops,[12] issued shortly after the second anti-Jewish law.[13] Paul Claudel, who was to stigmatize Cardinal Baudrillart's collaborationism at his death in 1942, was nonetheless an ardent supporter of Vichy. "France has been delivered after sixty years from the yoke of the liberal Catholic party (professors, lawyers, Jews, and Freemasons). The new government invokes God and has restored the Grande Chartreuse to the monks."[14] This was enough to justify serving the dictatorship if not the occupiers, and thus the acceptance of Vichy becomes completely understandable. For the mass of Catholics, the new regime was not only rebuilding France by putting an end to contemptible liberal democracy and monstrous secularism, but it was also participating in the war against communism. Would it be reasonable to sow obstacles on the path to the moral and spiritual regeneration of France solely because the Jews were its victims? Besides, wasn't purging the national body of elements foreign to it precisely an essential aspect of national rebirth?

In these circumstances, the silence of the Catholic Church cannot be cause for surprise. The assembly of cardinals and archbishops held in Lyon on August 31, 1940, was discreetly advised a few weeks in advance of the proposed first anti-Jewish law. It seems that on the basis of the argument presented by Cardinal Gerlier of Lyon, it was decided not to interfere with the government's positive work of reconstructing France. The assembly reaffirmed, as it was to do on numerous subsequent occasions, its loyalty to the established authorities and recognized the existence of a Jewish Question.[15] In reality, the meaning of the step that had been taken by the new regime could have escaped no one: the government was sounding out the Church on a question which, it might be feared at Vichy, was capable of provoking resistance. Nothing of the kind happened. By its absolute silence, the Church not only accepted the principles of action governing the opening stages of the national revolution, but also gave its blessing to the anti-Jewish laws.

For anyone who knew French Catholicism well from the inside, the Church's support of Vichy was not at all surprising. This was the case for the philosopher Yves Simon, a disciple of philosopher Jacques Maritain, who as early as 1936 had attacked the signatories of the manifesto of Henri Massis, referred to earlier. Simon, specialist in the thought of Saint Thomas Aquinas, very soon discovered one truth: militant antifascists were not well liked in the Church. Coincidentally, the progressive journal *Sept,* the voice of advanced French Dominicans, which had been noted for its anti-Franco positions, ceased publication in August 1937 for "financial reasons." To replace *Sept,* Simon participated in launching *Temps présent,* but very soon, as Maritain had foreseen, the new journal adopted a pro-Franco and pro-Munich stance.[16] In 1941, Simon, who had been a professor at the University of Notre Dame in Indiana since 1938, published in Montreal an extraordinary indictment of the permeation of the cultured levels of French society by fascism. With finesse, his book (*La Grande Crise de la République française*) presented evidence of the contamination of the Catholic world by Action Française, whose fascist leanings were clear to Simon: "Powerful throughout the intelligentsia, during the period we are describing, Action Française exercised nearly total control in Catholic intellectual circles. In those circles, declaring that you were a democrat meant consenting to being the object of ironic and contemptuous pity."[17] Throughout the 1930s, the young philosopher had contemplated with horror the positions adopted by a very large portion of French Catholic opinion, those who had nothing but praise and admiration for the German dictator. How could it be otherwise, since in these circles, "Hitler was the most fearsome adversary of Communism; he was an enemy of atheism and Freemasonry, he invoked God in his speeches."[18]

Perceptively, Yves Simon understood the place occupied by hatred in the worldview of the French right that came to power in 1940. In the first place, the "average French bourgeois" had been taught to hate the Jews: "In the course of the last few years before the war, antisemitic feeling made considerable progress in the French bourgeoisie, and the unspeakable racist decrees enacted by the Pétain government were not at all surprising to anyone who was aware of the situation."[19] Further, the abdication of the elite was explained by the settled belief in nationalist circles and among many Catholics that the true enemies of civilization were not the Nazis but the democrats, the Communists, and the Jews.[20] For Simon, as for Maritain, the right, out of hatred for democracy and the French Revolution, bore responsibility for the moral debacle and the advent of fascism. Maritain, for example, deplored the campaign in support of Vichy carried out by Father Garrigou-Lagrange in the *Revue universelle.* After the war, he made sure to recall that the distinguished Dominican, mentor of the future Pope John Paul II, had considered joining Charles de Gaulle to be a mortal sin. Like Simon, he was alarmed at the opportunism of the journal *Esprit,* which accepted the loss of freedom as a foregone conclusion.[21] But Yves Simon and Jacques Maritain were in the United States; in France the mass of Catholics chose Vichy. In these circumstances, since the anti-Jewish policy was dear to Pétain, since it was a policy that had at least the tacit support of the Church and was applied to the letter by the major institutions of the state, what chance of survival could the Michlins possibly have had?

When the persecutions began, Gilbert Michlin did not understand. He knew that not everyone liked the Jews. It was difficult, if you were ten at the time of the Popular Front, not to notice the anti-Semitic campaigns, the attacks against socialist premier Léon Blum and all the others with names that did not evoke French soil. It was hard to ignore the mass demonstrations against foreigners, also directed primarily against the Jews. The constant pressure exercised by Action Française and the other leagues, the imposing processions of the Croix-de-Feu, and the posters covering the walls of Paris that denounced the presence of *métèques* (a derogatory term for immigrants) were the daily fare. Gilbert Michlin knew that, despite their efforts, his parents, his uncle Albert, and his cousin Mayer were not entirely like the others. But he could not imagine that these people could constitute a "Jewish Question," or that they might have any responsibility for the misfortunes that had befallen the country, and hence that there could be any reason to subject them to discriminatory treatment.

During the three-and-a-half years separating the entry of the Germans into Paris and his deportation, Gilbert Michlin dealt exclusively with the French authorities. The French laws of October 1940 and June 1941 established the legal basis for exclusion, and the French police applied them. His father, who was out of work after the closing of Mayer Elina's workshop, went to work as a logger in les Landes in the spring of 1941. He was arrested early in 1942 by the French police and interned in the camp of Mérignac-Beaudésert in accordance with the law on foreigners. However, it is the date of the arrest of Gilbert and his mother that is most striking; on the night of February 3, 1944, two uniformed police officers pounded on their door. When a French prisoner asked him for news of the country on his arrival at Birkenau, Gilbert told him that there was talk of an Allied invasion. During the roundups of July 1942, it was still possible to believe in German victory. Collaboration with the enemy, cemented by handing over to the occupying forces political refugees and Jews who had come to France well before the rise of Nazism, could still be explained by the wish to stay on the good side of the new masters of Europe. But this was no longer the case in February 1944. In 1942, at the height of Nazi power, the transport "to an unknown destination" of four thousand children whom the Germans did not want, but who had become a burden for the French government because they were separated from their parents, could fit into the logical framework of collaboration. The situation was entirely different in early 1944. We can see most clearly now both the intrinsic importance of the anti-Jewish policy and the acceptability of that policy for large sectors of public opinion. At that time, no one thought that they would be called to account one day. And in fact, they were not.

The hunting of the Jews was of such importance that it allowed for no exceptions. Six months after Gilbert and his mother were arrested, seven officers of the local police precinct, which had shortly before been turned into a departure point for Auschwitz, died for the liberation of Paris. In February as in August 1944, these policemen who scrupulously executed the policies of René Bousquet, general secretary of the national police, and his delegate in the occupied zone, Jean Leguay, were persuaded that they were serving the nation well. These men were not cowards, and if they did not make the simple gesture of warning or helping those who were condemned to deportation, this was not because their courage failed them or because they were forced into it by the occupier. They were good French patriots. However, not only were the Jews of no interest to them, but in addition, the administrative hierarchy had explained to them that by helping to rid the country of those undesirables, human beings of inferior quality or of a different species, they were working for its salvation. This was indeed the logic of the National Revolution. Attributing the operation of the machinery of exclusion and then of extermination to a simple sequence of bureaucratic events, as some French historians prefer to do, is another form of suppression. The fact that the administrative wheels functioned so well does not mean that they moved all by themselves. Behind them lay the driving force of a solid, well-rooted ideology and a clear political will. Certainly, it was not the regime of the National Revolution that took the initiative to exterminate Jews. But it certainly did take the initiative in excluding and incarcerating foreigners in concentration camps. In doing so, the French government seized the opportunity not only to seal its

alliance with the victor but also to achieve one of its most important goals: to get rid of the maximum number of Jews, to exclude
the others from public life, and to change irrevocably the character
of French society.

Less than three months after the fall of the republic, the first
anti-Jewish legislation was enacted, indicating the importance
Vichy attributed to the law of October 1940 (Statute on the Jews).
One wonders why we had to wait for Robert Paxton's 1972 book,
Vichy France: Old Guard and New Order, 1940–1944), to learn that
this legislation owed nothing to any intervention by the conqueror.
After all, only the desire to conceal reality can explain the fact that
the conclusions were not reached earlier. At the trial of Raphaël
Alibert, the justice minister responsible for the first law, the charge
of complicity with the enemy had to be abandoned, because there
had never been the slightest trace of any connection between him
and the occupation authorities. Similarly, at his High Court trial,
Xavier Vallat, commissioner of Jewish affairs, used the following
defense in speaking of the second anti-Jewish law of 1941: "Never,
never did I base the Statute on the Jews on foreign models. Not at
all. I reconnected across the ages with national traditions and the
traditions of Christendom."[22] Vallat, famous for his furious attacks
against Premier Léon Blum, was speaking the simple truth, if not a
banality. This is clear to anyone who has read Barrès and Maurras,
Le Bon and Drumont, to name only the most famous and two of
the best-selling writers of their time, or who has glanced at the
Catholic press during the Dreyfus Affair and in the 1930s, or who
has leafed through the enormous quantity of popular newspapers
like Henri Rochefort's *L'Intransigeant, La Croix,* and its countless
provincial counterparts, or Coty's *L'Ami du peuple,* not to mention
L'Action Française or *Je suis partout.* The French laws were harsher
than the Nuremberg laws, not to mention the Italian racial laws,
which were never applied with the same rigor as in France. In fact,
Italian laws permitted an escape from the definition of "Jew" by
conversion to Catholicism, and there were examples in Italian-
occupied territory of the army, civil servants, and leaders of the
Fascist National Party organizing to protect Jews. On the other

hand, in France, the racial laws provoked no form of active resistance, from either the elite or ordinary men, principally civil servants, who were in a position to come to the aid of the condemned.

It is important to emphasize the point. The 1940 laws against the Jews—French Jews on October 3, foreign Jews on October 4, and the Jews of North Africa on October 7—constitute a cornerstone of the National Revolution. By excluding French Jews from the national community, and by herding foreign Jews into concentration camps and turning them over to the enemy, the men who came to power in the summer of 1940 made their position clear beyond any doubt. They defined the nation in terms made famous by Maurice Barrès, the preeminent ideologue of the anti-Dreyfusards, the theoretician of Earth and the Dead, of Blood and Soil. This definition is how the new regime intended to answer one of the great questions of our time, a truly existential question, for the fate of the Jews has depended on the answer that has been given to it over the course of the last two centuries: "What is a nation?" Is it a group of citizens, a collection of individuals who feel bound together by a common fate or a common culture or, conversely, is it a large family, a tribe huddled around its churches and its cemeteries, and communing in the cult of its ancestors? What are the criteria for national belonging? Are they objective, historical, ethnic, racial, and religious, or the freely expressed will of individuals? Is it conceivable that a nation can be built on the idea of a social contract? Put another way, is being a French citizen and belonging to the French nation one and the same? Is every citizen of France necessarily French? Are some less French than others? Is French identity defined in political and legal terms, or is it on the contrary a product of ethnic, biological, or racial factors? Can people who are not united by blood ties participate in the same cultural heritage and enjoy the same rights?

One answer was given in September 1791, when the French Revolution granted citizenship to the Jews. A second answer came with the racial laws of 1940: to rank as a French citizen had become a mere legal fiction. In fact, with the establishment of the dictatorship, all of the French ceased being citizens and became subjects of a dictator, but the situation of the Jews had become tragic, because their citizenship was the only bond that could have insured their safety and often their survival. For foreign Jews, from the beginning it was a question of life and death. However, the anti-Jewish law was far from being an improvisation. Its provisions had been set out in the program of the nationalist, Catholic, anti-Enlightenment right since the last decade of the nineteenth century. We can thus understand why Vichy was neither an expedient nor the product of mere opportunism, and why it did not come out of an ideological void. The National Revolution was the culmination of a long tradition, for France had produced not only a rationalist, universalist, and humanist political tradition, but also its antithesis—organicist, particularist, and anti-rationalist. In fact, it would not be difficult to write the intellectual history of France since the Revolution as an endless confrontation between these two concepts of the political good, these two philosophies of history. The major crisis, which in many ways marked the beginning of the French twentieth century, the Dreyfus Affair, is a striking example of this, and it clearly shows the continuity of the two traditions. The affair, involving a false conviction of treason against Alfred Dreyfus, a French military officer and Jew, became a major national political issue, pitting the Church, royalists, militarists, and anti-Semites against the Dreyfusards (republicans, socialists, and anticlerical groups). It was not just a simple confrontation between good and evil. It was a battle between two conceptions of society, morality, and politics. At the turn of the twentieth century, it marked the high point of the effort to destroy the intellectual foundations of democracy. The outcome of the conflict was a victory for the supporters of universal principles, but the potential for first cultural and then ethnic nationalism, for policy based on biological determinism, had been clearly demonstrated. For the losers of that battle and their intellectual heirs, the defeat of 1940 provided the opportunity to implement the principles they had advocated forty years earlier: Vichy was a moment at which the historicist, organicist, and particularist tradition resumed primacy.

Measures of repression, with their endless trail of misfortune and tragedy, all had the same purpose: to restore to the nation its organic unity, to replace once and for all the idea of a society conceived in terms of free citizens having equal rights with the theory of the organic solidarity of the nation. All the Vichy legislation that changed the face of the country in the six months following the Armistice—the establishment of the dictatorship, the implementation of a system of police repression, the cult of the charismatic leader, the reforms of the educational system, the organization of youth, censorship, the manipulation of news, the effort to impose a form of corporatism—all tended to restore to the nation its character as an organism analogous to a living being.

Throughout the twentieth century, there were many who thought that anyone could be made into a French citizen with a stroke of the pen, but that no one could transform the heart and soul of a Jew into a French heart and soul. No one could make a Jew into a descendant of the Crusaders; no one could make a Jew into a Celt. This is why the emancipation of the Jews by the French Revolution, the living symbol of the nation as an aggregate of individuals, was an act against nature that had to be abolished and all traces of it removed. The Jews had been liberated by virtue of the application of a universal principle. But for the men who came to power in 1940, as for those who had led the campaign against Dreyfus, universal principles did not exist.

The tragedy of the Jews, as Gilbert Michlin clearly saw, was theirs alone. The dominant feeling in the general population was indifference, fostered by the idea that the Jew was different, hence inferior. It was indeed this fundamental insensitivity, the product of broadly accepted ideology, that explains why the mechanism of destruction was able to function without a hitch almost to the very end. But the indifference to the fate of the Jews that Michlin came up against was ideological. When his mother, who expected the worst and knew that she had no way of escaping, even so asked for help from a friend, she confronted anti-Semitism. Contrary to the apologetic interpretation of the period, this was not a matter of mere apathy, but of half a century of anti-Semitism, literary, cultural, but also political. The anti-Semitism of wealthy neighborhoods and society salons, as well as of working-class suburbs and lower-class neighborhoods, had finally borne fruit.

What could be expected from ordinary people when the elite hastened to align themselves with the new regime? At the critical moment, when Renée Michlin brought her small suitcase containing personal things and her most precious souvenirs to the mother of Gilbert's great friend Maurice, Mme. Culet did not offer to hide Renée and her son in the country house in Saint-Maur. To do so she would have needed not only courage but also the profound conviction that Jews were human beings like any others, exposed to barbaric persecutions arising from a criminal policy. But Mme. Culet, the owner of a small hotel, was an ordinary Frenchwoman; she did not have a nonconformist mentality or the soul of a heroine. She had probably read in her newspaper throughout the 1930s, all jumbled together, not very gentle reflections on the Jewish invasion and on the inferiority of the Semitic race (an idea taken from nineteenth-century historian Ernest Renan and endlessly repeated since then), along with the axiom of Barrès that the Jews belonged not only to a different race ("that Dreyfus is capable of treason I deduce from his race") but to a different species.[23] If she were slightly more cultivated, she might have read in Maurras' *L'Appel au soldat* a passage that the nationalist, Catholic, and Maurrassian right had made into a veritable battle cry: "Every foreigner who has settled on our territory, even if he believes that he cherishes us, naturally hates eternal France, our tradition, which he does not possess, which he cannot understand, and which precisely constitutes nationality."[24]

Léon Daudet, editor of *Action Française,* had taught wide sectors of French public opinion, Catholic opinion first of all, that the Jew was, along with war and cholera, one of the three major scourges. The Jew lived from war and cholera: "Living by plunder, as a foreigner, a nomad, he loves the death of others as a profit. . . . Being himself a chronic plague and a permanent infection, he is on the same level as cholera."[25] These simple formulas, readily understood by a popular audience, captured their attention, and something of them always remained in people's minds. In addition, the essence of the principles on which the measures taken in October 1940 were based can be found in the Maurrassian bible, *Enquête sur la monarchie:* since there is "a Jewish Question" in France which is an "economic and ethnic question," it is fitting to resolve it not only through "strict economic and financial regulation," but by inaugurating "a complete review of citizenship and naturalization records."[26] In 1899, Maurras proposed that all Jews be treated as foreigners and that they therefore be prohibited from holding public office.[27] Already ten years earlier, during the Boulangist campaign, nationalists had found in anti-Semitism the perfect "popular formula."[28] From then on, the Jew bore responsibility not only for the death of Christ, but also for unemployment and poverty. The idea that French Jews could be stripped of citizenship was in the air at a time when France had a little more than one hundred thousand Jews.

For years, the attention of a large number of newspaper readers had been drawn to the excessive space occupied by Jews in political, cultural, and economic life. The same thing was true in Germany. Thomas Mann, one of the few intellectuals who eventually chose exile, still thought in the early years of Hitler's rule that the exclusion of Jews from political and cultural life, including de-Judaization of the justice system, for example, was not wrong in principle.[29] How could it have been otherwise in France, at the time of the Popular Front and then of the Munich agreement, when accusations against Jews, immigrants, and foreigners in general, all potential warmongers, had become commonplace? Saul Friedländer has clearly shown that in Germany the war against the Jews began with exclusion, a measure that did not seem to shock the moral conscience even of anti-Nazis like Mann, author of *The Magic Mountain.* Was the situation very different for the major artistic and literary figures in the country of Émile Zola and Anatole France?[30] At the turn of the twentieth century, France had given the world an unforgettable lesson in the Dreyfus Affair, but forty years later the "universal" intellectual, of whom Zola, that celebrated "moment of human conscience," has remained the prototype, was nowhere to be found. The great Dreyfusards, defenders of universal principles, had no heirs.

Moreover, a widespread idea held that the Jews themselves bore responsibility for anti-Semitism. This conviction was so deeply rooted that it resurfaced immediately after World War II in courses designed, after the ordeal, to educate the future elite in one of the most prestigious French institutions, the Institut d'Études Politiques ("Sciences Po") in Paris. Let us imagine for a moment that, instead of crossing the Atlantic, Gilbert Michlin had decided to remake his life in Paris. Suppose that he no longer wanted to be a toolmaker, but decided to pursue higher education in a selective school. Suppose that he wanted to be a prominent person—a public official, a university professor, or a major journalist—and for that purpose he signed up at Sciences Po. There he would have taken courses given by André Siegfried, president of the school's administrative council, professor at the Collège de France, elected to the Académie Française in October 1944, a leading figure in postwar intellectual life. Returning from the camps, Michlin would have heard how, following the best tradition of the first half of the twentieth century, this leading professor defined anti-Semitism as a defensive reflex in the face of the Jewish invasion. Summarizing the courses given by the member of the Académie and preparing for his final exams, Michlin would have learned that, now and forever, Jews alone bear the responsibility for anti-Semitism. In Germany, in an economic geography course given in 1947, it was stated that the Jews had conquered Berlin, where they had succeeded in occupying a preponderant place in economic and cultural life. From this, Siegfried concluded that "their role in Weimar was decisive, and Hitler's anti-Semitism was a reaction to that."[31] In a book published in 1950, with the suggestive title *l'Âme des peuples* (The Soul of the People), repeating the content of his courses, the famous political scientist continues his analysis: "We must speak again of the Jews, even after the massive persecution by Hitler." It is necessary to speak of the Jews in order to understand the events that the author euphemistically calls "the persecution we know about."[32] According to him, after World War I, a new kind of immigrant arrived in Berlin, "rather similar to the Jewish invasion of New York. They were to be found, so to speak, at the intersection of business and intelligence. Newspapers, theaters, the cinema, the antiques trade, medicine, and the courts tended more and more to belong to them."[33] In reading the founder of French political science, it is easy to come to the conclusion that Nazi anti-Semitism was the natural, almost legitimate, result of that invasion.

The same thing was true in the United States: anti-Semitism constituted a response to the Jewish "conquest." Whether they came from the aristocracy of London or Frankfurt or the ghettos of Poland or Ukraine, whether they changed their name from Schönberg to Belmont or from Jonas to Jones, Jews provoked the same kind of reactions. It was not merely a question of the strong competition they offered for good jobs, from the world of business to the universities, but also of the fact that, bound to one another by "racial ties," the Jews were unassimilable. In a natural way, they were said to have brought "the Protestant American to adopt a hostile attitude that has developed into an antisemitic movement."[34]

Professor Siegfried contended that the same thing was true in France. Anti-Semitism is explained in accordance with the same principle: in the last analysis, it is the Jewish soul that engenders a defensive reflex. André Siegfried, who always refers back to Barrès, sees the Jews through the eyes of the anti-Dreyfusard agitator.[35] In the notes for his course in 1957, he quotes Barrès to describe the Jewish temperament, their "nomad sensibility": "These Jewish minds . . . manipulate ideas the way a banker manipulates assets." Ideas for them are only "tokens that they sort out on a cold counter top." In the end, the Jew appears to him to be "a residue that cannot be fused in the crucible." This means that anti-Semitism is "not economic in nature," but "a doctrinal reaction against the Jewish approach to problems."[36] If analyses of this kind could be presented to a class of students in the years following the Liberation without provoking a reaction, they must have been part of a widespread body of accepted ideas.

It was precisely in order not to have to hear this kind of explanation, and especially not from a major university professor, that Gilbert Michlin left France. By October 1944, when Michlin was still in Birkenau fighting a daily battle merely to survive, the philosopher Gabriel Marcel, in an article published in *Témoignage chrétien*, was calling on the Jews as their persecution ended to be "discreet in their demands."[37] During the same period, André Weil-Curiel, who had spent the war years in London, gave a "young Jewish friend" this advice designed to enable him to resume a normal life: "Act so that the good French people of France who hoped never to see you again forget that you exist."[38] For more than half a century, the great majority of the Jews of France have conscientiously followed this advice.

Gilbert Michlin did not want to take part in this return to normality; he could not bear the idea that life could resume where it had left off on the eve of the October 1940 laws. He could not accept the thought that the chief of the Vichy police, the boss of the police who had picked up his mother, could be honored as a fighter of the Resistance. The fact that Jewish Resistance fighters, the deported, and the orphans (with a few exceptions, in the first rank of whom it is fitting to name Beate and Serge Klarsfeld) did not dare until the late 1990s to raise a great cry of protest, says a great deal about their feelings of solitude and isolation. The fact that the criminal court could dismiss the case against Paul Touvier in 1992, on the pretext that this *milicien* (member of a paramilitary force created within the veterans' legion) could not be tried for crimes against humanity, says a good deal about conventional thinking. By accepting the principle that the activities of the *milicien,* however ignoble they may have been, had not been carried out in the service of "a state practicing a policy of ideological hegemony," the three judges were saying that Vichy did not belong to the same type of regime as fascist Italy and Nazi Germany.[39] For them, it was merely a conservative regime, vaguely rank, and not a dictatorship. The tribunal thus associated itself with the work of repression undertaken by French historiography beginning immediately after the Liberation. The criminal court's decision, we know, was swept away by a wave of public outrage, but French students continue to learn in *lycées* and universities that for all those who hastened into the service of the national revolution, the Vichy regime recalled the kingdom of Bourges, and that "the association between the Maid and the Marshal" was self-evident.[40] That is not an idea that would have occurred to Gilbert Michlin on the night of February 3, 1944, when his mother opened the door to the faithful servants of the new kingdom of Bourges.

Michlin's fine narrative is the product of an experience, a faithful and precious testimony. It is the story of a Jewish family that did not have the good fortune of finding a Righteous person on its path, or of merely finding a charitable soul, a sensitive friend, a generous neighbor, a policeman who agreed not to knock on the door too loudly. If only Renée Michlin, who like the heroine of a Greek tragedy knew the fate that awaited her and resigned herself to it, had met someone to help her hold on for a few weeks longer! Others had more luck: three-quarters of the Jews of France survived. The fact that only twenty-one hundred French people have been recognized by Yad Vashem as "Righteous among the Nations" does not mean, as Gilbert Michlin says, that only twenty thousand Jews were saved by the population. If that had been the case, the fate of the Jews of France would have been comparable to that of the Jews of Poland—virtual extermination.

Every Jewish child who was able to overcome destiny had a different story, and yet each one's past always has a common element. The son of Moshe and Riwka Michlin did not have the same adventure as Saul Friedländer, who escaped from Czechoslovakia at the age of six, arrived in Paris on the eve of the war, and was hidden in the heart of rural France, in a boarding school that "brought up its pupils in a particularly strict Catholicism, even for the time, and encouraged, insofar as possible, vocations for the priesthood."[41] Handed over by his parents—who, like Michlin's mother, were beginning to lose hope of escaping from the net that was tightening around them—to the ladies of Solidarité, Friedländer survived, converted and assimilated into a quasi-royalist milieu that ardently supported Pétain. As the underground was liberating Montluçon, his circle still hated Gaullism and the Resistance. However, it had never occurred to anyone in this society, where the misdeeds of the Jews were recited during Holy Week, where the harangues of that sinister French Nazi Philippe Henriot were read every morning, and where his execution was experienced as a national tragedy, to play along with the racial laws. Baptized with everyone's knowledge in the Notre Dame church of Montluçon, Paul-Henri (Marie was added for the occasion) had ceased to be a Jew.

At the last moment, before trying to flee to Switzerland, Elli and Jan Friedländer had certainly understood that it was right not only to authorize the headmistress of the Saint-Béranger school to baptize their son, but also to promise her "to continue your work in

the path set forth by you, as soon as the will of God and the circumstances allow us to take care of his education ourselves."[42] They
had no illusion about their own fate: there was no one in their
Montluçon neighborhood who offered to help either the child or
his parents. However, in evoking those years when he changed from
Pavel or Pavlicek to Paul, and then to Paul-Henri Ferland (an ado-
lescent thrown on his own devices whose only emotional recourse
was to religion, and a brilliant student for whom a career as a Jesuit
was predicted), Saul Friedländer retains an emotional memory of all
those who helped him. He remembers "Mme. M. de L.," the librarian of Néris, toward whom his despairing mother had turned at the
last moment and who had found the solution of Saint-Béranger; his
three teachers; and the good Mme. Chancel, the headmistress of the
Montneuf school. Here and there, glimmers in the night. . . . But
reality is seldom simple, and in the course of those dark years it was
less simple than ever. When the *milice,* knowing what had happened to the parents, came looking for the child who might have
escaped, Mme. M. de L. faced up to them and once again protected
her young protégé from the fate that struck Gilbert Michlin at the
same moment. It was only at that point that we learn that Mme. M.
de L. was born Jewish.

Gilbert Michlin had a different experience. He has not a single positive memory, no act of humanity that he can look back on.
He was not Saul Friedländer or Isaac Lewendel, who was taken in
after his mother's arrest by a peasant family in Provence who treated
him as a member of the family.[43] Unlike Danièle Gervais-Marx, he
did not see the owners of a café in the village of Hauterives rescue
from a German soldier, who had just lost his son on the eastern
front, three Jewish children whose parents were being taken away.[44]
Nor did he hear the Alsatian woman say *O Jesus Gott* on her return
from the camp of Drancy to which she had just taken a food parcel.
Having witnessed the suffering of the children, this woman who
had attended mass every Sunday of her life broke out in sobs:
"There is no God!" Like Saul Friedländer twenty years ago, and like
Isaac Lewendel and Danièle Gervais-Marx more recently, Gilbert
Michlin has recreated his experience. But there is a difference: like
most of the Jews who survived, those other children of the Shoah

owe their lives both to themselves and to others, the Righteous among the Nations, men and women to whom we Jews have contracted a debt that will never be repaid. They saw evil, but they also saw good. On the other hand, Gilbert Michlin knows that his mother did not even have the final consolation that lightened the last moments of Saul Friedländer's parents: the knowledge that their only son was in another place. Gilbert Michlin owes his life only to himself, to his physical strength and his moral capacities. He saw hell in its pure state.

Gilbert Michlin has written to testify about what he saw and what he felt and still feels, even after his return at the pinnacle of a successful career to live in Paris, the city of his childhood that he loves, now and always. This account is about the 75,721 deported Jews, of whom only 3 percent returned. Those women, those men, and those children were not only victims of Nazism but also of fascism in its French variety. The former slave of Siemens wants responsibilities to be clearly established. He wants us to recognize that there never was a Jewish Question, but only a French question. For the France of the second half of the twentieth century, the Vichy dictatorship and its racial laws raised the fundamental question of French singularity. Could it seriously be claimed that France, as the national consensus would have it, had been immunized once and for all by its republican tradition against the *mal du siècle* embodied by fascism? Or, was it not rather more appropriate to ask whether it had not produced a national variant of that form of supreme revolt against the Enlightenment? Wasn't the France of the turn of the twentieth century, precisely because it was the most advanced liberal society in Europe, the real laboratory of ideas in which the fascist synthesis was forged? The idea that Vichy was the result of a long process of incubation, that those years everyone wanted to forget belonged to national history just as much as the ages of greatness, was an unbearable thought for an entire generation.

Even more difficult to accept is the idea that, compared to Italian fascism, the Vichy regime was the more bloodthirsty. The Italian occupation zone was a refuge for the Jews of France, and fascist Italy—its police, its soldiers, and its officials, led by its diplomats—protected foreign as well as Italian Jews against the French authorities. Conversely, the French government saw the saving of Jews by Italians operating on its territory as a breach of its sovereignty. In some respects, the Vichy regime was closer to the Nazi than to the Italian fascist dictatorship. This is why historians made extraordinary efforts for half a century not only to dissociate French society from Vichy and to erase the National Revolution from the history of France, but also quite bluntly to cover up its crimes. Vichy had to disappear from national consciousness, and the epic of Free France and the Resistance had to become the story of all of France. It was vital for the rebirth of postwar France that Free France be, as de Gaulle saw so clearly, quite simply *la France*.

A new generation has now arrived. Unlike their parents and grandparents who wanted to forget or conceal the past, this generation wants to know. Hence, thinking about the fate suffered by the Jews of France during World War II has been transformed. Jews are speaking out and calling society and the government to account. They are taking the liberty of asking questions that were in the past almost unthinkable, and they demand answers. This new generation insisted on putting Paul Touvier and Maurice Papon on trial and demanded that the ceremony of placing flowers at Pétain's tomb be abandoned. The words used by François Mitterrand in 1994, when he refused to accept responsibility in the name of France for the crimes of Vichy or when he claimed to have known nothing of the racial laws and denied his friendship with Bousquet, have become unacceptable for this generation. Mitterrand did not understand that society had changed. The last remaining war criminals are dying off, but the historical debate is only beginning.

The experience that Gilbert Michlin lived through calls forth one final thought. The history of those years, during which our brilliant and cultured Europe was the most horrible place on the surface of the earth, demonstrates that we should forget neither the great precariousness of the Jewish condition nor the fragility of principles and traditions that seem to belong to the natural order of things. In the summer of 1940, democracy, freedom, and human rights collapsed in France like a house of cards. This shows us that no society, no matter what its history, no matter how great its contribution to what Benedetto Croce called the history of freedom, is immunized against the forces of destruction that are an integral part of our civilization, now as in the past. To be sure, it was military defeat that set the National Revolution in motion, but defeat itself did not necessitate the installation of a fascist dictatorship. The same thing holds for Italy and Germany. Their defeat of 1918, unemployment, and inflation, do not alone explain the rise of fascism and Nazism, nor does the Soviet revolution for that matter. The disaster was possible because the economic and social crisis was combined with intellectual and moral anguish. Too many people in Europe had been deeply convinced for too long of the moral and intellectual inferiority of the rationalist, universalist, and humanist culture of the Enlightenment, preferring in its place the tribal culture of nationalism, blood, and soil.

Never before, it seems, had the truth that shone forth in Europe in the 1930s and 1940s been seen so clearly: everywhere in the world, the fate of the Jews was tied to the fate of universal values. More than any other community, more than any other social group, their history had for two centuries been dependent on the survival of the open society that is the legacy of the Enlightenment. The existence of the Jews could be guaranteed in only two kinds of society: Jews could survive under the Ancien Régime, where they were one corporate body among others, a society in which each social group possessed specific rights and duties that were recognized as such; and they could survive in a society that adopted the universal principle of the equality of all human beings, with no distinctions of race, religion, or ethnic origin. Conversely, the Jews could not survive in a society thought of as a body, a tribe, or an extended family, a society of blood and soil, of earth and the dead. This is why the war waged against the legacy of the eighteenth century was also, often primarily, a war against the Jews, and the catastrophe of the Jews of Europe was the result of the most extreme forms of the war waged against an entire civilization founded on the values of the Enlightenment.

Notes

1. Renée Poznanski, *Etre juif en France pendant la Seconde Guerre mondiale* (Paris: Hachette, 1994), 23–24.

2. Maurice Barrès, "Les diverses familles spirituelles de la France—les Israélites," *L'Écho de Paris,* December 11 and 15, 1916. Between November 27, 1916, and March 9, 1917, Barrès published twenty articles on "various spiritual families," religious and secular. The articles were published as a book with that title in 1917. After the promulgation of the anti-Jewish laws of 1940, Jews often appealed to the memory of the Barrès of the "Spiritual Families" to evoke their patriotism and their service to the country.

3. First place was given to Gustave Hervé, a revolutionary socialist agitator who had become a vulgar chauvinist.

4. Palestine was under British mandate from the end of World War I until the proclamation of the State of Israel in 1948.

5. Pierre Birnbaum, *Les Fous de la République* (Paris: Fayard, 1992), 448ff.

6. Decree granting French citizenship to the Jews of Algeria proposed by the deputy Isaac Crémieux in 1870.

7. Robert Badinter, opening remarks in *Il y a cinquante ans: Le Statut des juifs de Vichy,* ed. Serge Klarsfeld (Paris: CDJC, 1991), 11.

8. Pierre Assouline, *Le Dernier des Camondo* (Paris: Le Grand Livre du mois, 1997), 272.

9. Jacques Duquesne, *Les Catholiques français sous l'Occupation* (Paris: Seuil, 1996), 181.

10. Emmanuel Mounier, "Fin de l'homme bourgeois," *Esprit,* July 1941, 611.

11. Ibid., 609.

12. Duquesne, *Les Catholiques français sous l'Occupation,* 61.

13. The first law defining the Jew was promulgated in October 1940.

14. Quoted in Jean-Pierre Azéma, *De Munich à la Libération* (Paris: Seuil, 1979), 103. The Grande Chartreuse in the French Alps is the seat of a most austere Catholic order of French monks, founded in 1084. The order was expelled from France in 1903.

15. Pierre Laborie, "Le statut des juifs et l'opinion française," in Klarsfeld, *Il y a cinquante ans,* 87 (see note 7).

16. John Hellman, introduction to *The Road to Vichy, 1918–1938,* by

Yves R. Simon (Lanham, MD: University Press of America, 1988), vii–xi.

17. Yves Simon, *La Grande Crise de la République française. Observations sur la vie politique des Français de 1918 à 1938* (Montreal: Éditions de l'Arbre, 1941), 52.

18. Ibid., 107.

19. Ibid., 175. It is interesting to note that Yves Simon could not imagine that the racial laws were not imposed by the conqueror.

20. Ibid., 192ff.

21. Hellman, introduction to *The Road to Vichy,* xviii–xxii.

22. Quoted by Robert Badinter, opening remarks in Klarsfeld, *Il y a cinquante ans,* 12.

23. I take the liberty of referring here to the new edition of my book, *Maurice Barrès et le nationalisme français* (Paris: Fayard, 2000), 294ff.

24. Maurice Barrès, *L'Appel au soldat* (Paris: Fasquelle, 1900), 178.

25. Quoted in Colette Capitan-Peter, *Charles Maurras et l'idéologie d'Action française* (Paris: Seuil, 1972), 76.

26. Charles Maurras, *Enquête sur la monarchie* (Paris: Librairie Arthème Fayard, n.d.), 62.

27. Capitan-Peter, *Charles Maurras et l'idéologie d'Action française,* 77.

28. Barrès, *L'Appel au soldat,* 465.

29. Saul Friedländer, *Nazi Germany and the Jews,* vol. 1, *The Years of Persecution, 1933–1939* (New York: HarperCollins, 1997), 11.

30. Ibid., 118ff.

31. Quoted in Pierre Birnbaum, *"La France aux Français" in Histoire des haines nationalistes* (Paris: Seuil, 1993), 154.

32. André Siegfried, *L'Âme des peuples* (Paris: Hachette, 1950), 118.

33. Ibid., 119–20.

34. André Siegfried, *America Comes of Age. A French Analysis* (New York: Harcourt, Brace, 1927), 25–27.

35. See my *Maurice Barrès et le nationalisme français.*

36. Quoted in Birnbaum, *"La France aux Français,"* 149–50.

37. Gabriel Marcel, "Lendemain de persécution," *Témoignage chrétien,* October 21, 1944. This article is quoted by Henry Rousso, *Le Syndrome de Vichy* (Paris: Seuil, 1987), 135, as well as by Poznanski, *Etre juif en France,* 671 (see note 1).

38. Poznanski, *Etre juif en France,* 671 (see note 1).

39. "La milice, auxiliaire des services publics," *Le Monde,* April 15, 1992, 10.

40. René Rémond, *Notre siècle de 1918 à 1991* (Paris: Librairie générale française, 1993), 263. During the fifteenth century, Charles VII, King of Bourges, became King of France thanks to Joan of Arc (the Maid), who had defeated the English. A parallel is drawn: all those rallied to the cause of the National Revolution are symbolized by the Maid, while the Vichy regime personified by Marshal Pétain becomes the King of Bourges.

41. Saul Friedländer, *Quand vient le souvenir* (Paris: Seuil, 1978), 80.

42. Ibid., 78.

43. Isaac Lewendel, *Un hiver en Provence* (Paris: Éditions de l'Aube, 1996).

44. Danièle Gervais-Marx, *La Ligne de démarcation* (Paris: HB Éditions, 1997).